THE ART OF BEING A

BRILLIANT
NQT

GARY TOWARD AND CHRIS HENLEY
EDITED BY ANDY COPE

Crown House Publishing Limited
www.crownhouse.co.uk

First published by
Crown House Publishing
Crown Buildings, Bancyfelin, Carmarthen, Wales, SA33 5ND, UK
www.crownhouse.co.uk
and
Crown House Publishing Company LLC
6 Trowbridge Drive, Suite 5, Bethel, CT 06801-2858, USA
www.crownhousepublishing.com

© Gary Toward and Chris Henley, 2015

Illustrations © Amy Bradley, 2015

First published 2015.

British Library of Cataloguing-in-Publication Data
A catalogue entry for this book is available from the British Library.

Print ISBN 978-184590940-6
Mobi ISBN 978-184590945-1
ePub ISBN 978-184590946-8
ePDF ISBN 978-184590947-5

Edited by Andy Cope

LCCN 2015930350

Printed and bound in the UK by
Gomer Press, Llandysul, Ceredigion

CONTENTS

FOREWORD

Free-range education

Does anyone ever read the foreword? In this particular case, please do …

As well as being a student of the relatively new discipline of 'positive psychology' (the science of happiness and well-being), I also masquerade as a children's author. That means I get to do loads of school visits. More often than not, I arrive at 9 a.m. (which is a bad time to arrive at any school), sign in and hang about in reception while parents fluster around paying trip money to the receptionist behind the glass. Late and unkempt children are rushed through the door and I sit, trying to get my name badge to stick on, while I wait for whomever.

'Whomever' eventually arrives. They are always lovely. Stressed but lovely. And occasionally I catch a natter with the head teacher before my gig begins, but they are busy people so it's rare.

Except, just occasionally, that doesn't happen. You can sniff something a little bit different from the moment you arrive. You are ushered into the head's office while someone grabs you a coffee. You are alone – in the head's office! *Yikes!* And you can't help but notice there is a big blue box file marked 'Cunning plans' on the shelf. *Like it!* There is a wall crammed with postcards and thank-you notes from kids and parents. *Like it a lot!* You inspect the pin-board and there is a picture of a bloke and some kids playing didgeridoos. *Like it a very lot!*

And then the door explodes open and the didgeridoo bloke breezes in and shakes your hand so firmly you hear something crunch. He's the bloody head teacher! And he's closely followed by some sort of luvvie who grins and pumps your hand up and down while spouting all sorts of 'Carry On' double-entendres.

Welcome to Gary and Chris's world. Combined classroom experience of 150 years (just kiddin', chaps) and *still* with bags of enthusiasm, energy and the right amount of quirkiness. It's hard not to like them (believe me, I have tried) but, more importantly, it's impossible not to respect what they have achieved and what they stand for.

Education has been through some tough times in recent years. As someone just starting out in the teaching profession, it won't have escaped your notice that there are all sorts of goings on in schools – rumblings and mutterings that sometimes erupt into something a bit shouty on *Question Time*. And the BBC always reports on the national NUT conference, where the biggest teaching union seems intent on portraying teaching as the career from hell.

And, to be candid, I used to be a bit critical of the teaching profession. I had a 'proper job', you see. I delivered training for companies, which was all very important, grown-up and responsible of me. And my job allowed just four weeks' holiday. Imagine, four measly weeks. So the grumbling educationalists got on my wick. I would roll my eyes whenever the annual union foot-stamper banged on about terrible pay, conditions and pensions. I used to luxuriate in the irony that bullying is outlawed in schools yet these teachers thought it was perfectly fine to boo and heckle the secretary of state for education. In fact, they were so badly bullied that eventually they stopped turning up at the conferences. That was until I started delivering my workshops in schools. I soon realised that it was, on a conservative estimate, ten times more challenging than a corporate day. And also (on a good day) ten times more rewarding. I have come to appreciate the sheer workload of teachers and teaching assistants. This book sets out to be inspirational and positive, but I may as well tell you up front, teaching is a physically and emotionally exhausting profession.

Over the last few years, I have metamorphosed into one of the shouty people, a defender and champion of those in education. And I have come to a few stark realisations.

First, there is a chasm between an awesome teacher and a standard teacher. I guess there are chasms in all jobs, but teaching is probably where it shows the most (and maybe heart surgeons).

Second, it matters. The job of teaching really and truly matters. You are not manufacturing widgets in a factory or scanning Sunny Delight at Sainsbury's; you are shaping the lives of young people. I'm struggling to think of anything more crucial.

Third, I have yet to meet a teacher who comes to work to do a bad job. I doubt there is a single one who wakes up thinking, 'I'm determined to have a real stinker today.' Teachers want to be awesome. They are, almost without exception, motivated and passionate about their work.[1]

The problem is that the system is getting in the way of teachers being brilliant. The 'system' (Ofsted, rules, procedures, safeguarding, discipline, paperwork, marking, schemes of work, lesson plans, peer observations, risk assessments, targets, etc.) has been designed to stop poor teachers being poor. It is there to catch the bad ones, but the problem is that it also clips the wings of the good ones.

And then there is every teacher's favourite bugbear, the 'c' word: *change*. Most folks are willing and able to change if they have some say in it or see the sense of it, but the closer I've got to the teaching profession, the more I see that many of the changes are imposed and pointless. The result is exhaustion, stress, burnout and, in some cases, serious illness. Hence the ranty foot-stampers.

So, how do Gary and Chris maintain their youthful ebullience and sparkling repartee when others fall by the wayside? That is a very big question, but the short answer is they 'get it'; the 'it' being an understanding that it's all about relationships and feelings. They understand that if a teacher (or an entire school) can create an environment where pupils want to come to school, because it's such an awesome experience, then there

---

1 I say 'almost' because I once met a business studies teacher who had 'DILLIGAF?' written on his register. When I asked him what it meant, he explained, 'Do I Look Like I Give A F***?'

will be giant leaps of learning. Indeed, the difference between *wanting* to come to school and *having* to come to school is the 'it'.

Chris and Gary acknowledge the importance of league tables and targets but realise that, rather than browbeating children with the literacy and numeracy stick, you are more likely to achieve your targets if the learners feel respected, involved and inspired. And that is summed up in one word – engagement. If you boil this book down to its bare bones, it's all about engagement. I think that might be the 'it' again.

As an outsider looking in, I suspect that many teachers are so focused on their targeted results that the system has become more important than the students. It's the educational equivalent of battery farming, and the result is pretty much the same. Most schools are doing just fine; they follow the standardised, neatly packaged formula that churns out results. Teachers work inexorably harder, kids are pushed until the pips squeak, that's just the way it is. And that's fine if all you want to achieve is 'fine'.

But this book is called *The Art of Being a Brilliant NQT*. It's designed to take you into the rarefied atmosphere of 'world class'. But to be world class you have to dare to be a little bit different. And it can be hard to dare when the stakes are so high. Isn't it safer (and easier) to do what all the other teachers are doing?

Probably. But think of this book as the free-range approach to education. Farmers know that to get the best eggs, the chooks need to roam freely and explore. They need space and fresh air. The hens are happier and, hey presto, the eggs are much better quality.

I reckon this book will set you up to be a free-range teacher. Stretch your legs, stretch your mind, stretch your limits. We know that happy children produce their best work. Guess what? So do happy teachers!

Andy Cope

(Andy is a best-selling author and international speaker. He is on his way to becoming the UK's first ever 'Doctor of Happiness'. And, yes, that title does make him cringe.)

INTRODUCTION

Welcome to arguably the best job in the world. The pair of us often debate whether it's teaching or the medical profession that might be the most *important* job in the world. But the *best* job, for us, has to be teaching. Seeing the long term development and success of those you nurture. Watching the light bulb shine as a student suddenly 'gets it'. Having that inner sense of pride when you know you have made a difference in someone's life for the better. Even better, getting a pint bought for you by an ex-student who valued your support a few years earlier. Okay, we're really only in it for the beer! In actual fact, that does sort of sum it up. We've both lost count of how many pints we've been bought over the years, including at a reunion last year of Gary's first tutor group from 1983!

What we want you to do is be proud. Be proud of your profession. Be proud of your role and your contribution to the lives of youngsters. We want you to sidestep the people our mate, Andy Cope (the fella who wrote the foreword), calls mood-hoovers – you know, the moaning media, the groaning government and those glass half-empty colleagues who really shouldn't be in the job. We want you to be super-teachers and to whirl into your classroom like men and women possessed, inspiring all who cross your path. We're going to give you lots of top tips and little gems of wisdom that will make you feel like you're wearing your pants on the outside!

Before we begin, here's a thought. You are a newly qualified teacher. So let's draw a link to what you might be thinking when you confront a new intake at your school. You will be looking at them and wondering just how much learning you can stuff into them to help them become the best they can be. We're sitting here peering out of the page at you right now doing exactly the same thing. How good can you be? How far can you go? Have you thought that there is a career here with the potential of school leadership somewhere along the line? You might be aiming to become a brilliant teacher, but you might also step onto the right path to become a curriculum leader, assistant head or special educational needs coordinator. Whatever it is, we are going to help you get there. We will point you in the right direction to be able to shout, 'Pick me!', when it comes to promotions or career opportunities.

Still with us? Good. Before we get into the real nitty-gritty, here is our first top tip section. We like lists, as do most kids, which is why you are going to find plenty of them scattered throughout these pages. And, as for our style, don't expect a heavy textbook type tome here. We know you have a busy life and haven't got time to be wading through the statistics, government white papers or what the research shows from this or that university. Don't get us wrong, though, those books do have their place (Gary's got two holding his office door open), but this book is about what, in our experience, works. It's full of stuff that you can use on a daily basis to make your teaching both enjoyable and successful; stuff that you can't pick up from a textbook or a course.

There is nearly seventy years of combined experience here to help you. Put differently, that means over 50,000 lessons. We also want you to laugh. In fact, that is our first top tip: laugh with the kids. Have fun with them. If you can blur the lines between having fun and learning, then what you get is great learning.

TOP TIPS

FOR STARTING YOUR CAREER IN TEACHING

♦ Get in early! Whatever your start time, make sure you arrive with plenty of time. You can get a cuppa, check out the day ahead, do a bit of networking and be ready to go on the 'B' of the bell. Not only that, you will send great signals to the head teacher.

♦ You have a stressful job so plan ahead to reduce stress. We had a colleague once who thought he could do without a diary. Oddly, he went down like a lead balloon with colleagues as he constantly forgot what he had to do and where he should be. Plan, plan, plan and stick to your routines.

- Did we say it was stressful? Like lots of teachers, you will want to stay late to mark and plan. Make sure you give yourself at least one night when you leave by 4 p.m. and do not go home and work. As above, try to stick to your rule.

- Get a buddy. Find someone who you think you can learn from and work with (not a mood-hoover). There is nothing like sharing ideas, finding solutions and the general banter you can have with a good colleague. (Besides, when you decide to leave, you will need someone to organise the collection for your present!)

- Join in. Get involved in activities outside of the classroom – for example, a staff do, the parent–teacher association or a school fair. It will give you opportunities to develop relationships with colleagues who you may find it hard to meet during the normal school day, and it shows that you want to be part of the fabric of the school.

Finally, here is the biggie: the number one crucial thing you need to get right if you want to be successful in teaching. We can sum it up by saying it's all about relationships, but here is the quote that defines everything about what we think great teachers are like:

> I've come to the frightening conclusion that I am the decisive element in the classroom. It's my personal approach that creates the climate. It's my daily mood that makes the weather. As a teacher I possess a tremendous power to make a child's life miserable or joyous. I can be a tool of torture or an instrument of inspiration. I can humiliate or humor, hurt or heal. In all situations, it is my response that decides whether a crisis will be escalated or de-escalated, and a child humanized or de-humanized.
>
> Haim Ginott[2]

Read that quote? We suggest you read it again. Look at those words; the power in them. Get it wrong and you can destroy confidence and future aspirations. Get it right and, boy, you are a brilliant teacher. When we run our NQT courses our delegates tell us just how fired up they are to 'make a difference'. Well, this says it all: 'joyous … inspiration … humor … heal … de-escalate … humanized'. These are the traits of a teacher who helps to create the lives and the futures of young people. We want you to aspire to do that.

---

1   Haim Ginott, *Teacher and Child: A Book for Parents and Teachers* (New York: Macmillan, 1971).

It's unlikely you ever saw the 1970s TV series called *Columbo*, with Peter Falk playing a bugging eccentric investigator. Just when his suspects thought he had finished his questioning, he would turn back with one last thing to ask. If you didn't see it, there is bound to be an episode on the internet. They are worth a watch, at least once, as you can use some of his questioning techniques in the classroom.

So here's our Columbo-style, one last thing: in the teaching profession, we call the focus of our attention by all sorts of names – students, pupils, youngsters, kids. The latter is an interesting one. Kids. We once met someone who thought it was derogatory. We say, get a life! It's a term of endearment, in our view, so use it without fear, as teaching is all about kids! Sometimes what we call our learners formally is dictated by the age we teach; sometimes it's down to the tradition of the school. As there is no fixed code, we are going to use them all here.

Just be brilliant!

Chapter 1

GETTING INTO YOUR CAREER

A finger in the wind!

There are thousands of schools out there; a pick 'n' mix of every flavour of educational establishment waiting for the right teachers. Let's not be too hasty though. You may well be qualified, you may well have had a great year achieving your NQT status, but this is a buyer's market. Good teachers are hot property, so if you fall into that category, or have the potential to be good or outstanding, you can shop around.

So, it's worthwhile setting out how to choose your best-fit school, as well as how to apply and how to approach your interview. We acknowledge that a lot of this information is fairly straightforward; however, over the years, we have discovered that 'common sense' is by no means 'common practice'.

First, let's get the types of school sorted. The pick 'n' mix metaphor really is true. Never before have there been so many different types of school, so you need to know what you are getting yourself into before you accept a job and sign a contract. We are assuming you are sharp enough to know the difference between nursery, primary and secondary schools and the different permutations within those phases. Even so, watch out. Some areas have strange versions of these, with middle schools starting at Year 6 or Year 8 and primaries ending at Year 5. It's crucial that you check this out to make sure it's really what you want.

So, just to make sure you are fully equipped before we go any further, here is a summary of the main types of schools in the UK at the time of writing.

Local authority schools

These schools come in all phases and are monitored by the local authority. These used to be called local education authorities and, no doubt, will be called that again in good time. One thing you will find out about education, if you stick around long enough, is that there are few new ideas and we often return to the past wrapped up in shiny new packaging. These schools employ teachers via the local authority, with pay and conditions of service managed by the authority's human resources department, usually at something called County Hall or City Hall. Typically, salaries, working days and holiday patterns for these schools have been agreed across the entire local area. If you have children of your own, it's always worth checking term times to avoid finding yourself in a job where your kids have different holidays to you; a childcare nightmare!

However, there are differences even within local authorities because some schools have a structure that has been inherited from former grant maintained status. These schools were some of the first to be autonomous and not beholden to the local authority, and, as a result, many have retained the role of 'employer' themselves (actually it's the governors of the school – more about them in Chapter 9). In the grand scheme of things, this shouldn't be a worry, but it's worth finding out if the school follows local pay and conditions or not.

Academies

An academy school is a state school that has opted out of local authority control and become a charitable trust. Often the clue is in the name – for example, the Frank Evans Academy – but not always; some schools that have converted to academy status retain their original name or invent a new one. As with the old grant maintained schools, it's the governors who are the employers of academy staff. They are responsible for setting the school's pay and conditions of service and have a huge degree of autonomy in this area. If you apply for a job at an academy, make sure you check this out. Most will follow the local plan, but in some cases there are radically different conditions of service with unusual holiday patterns and/or working hours.

Academies can also be part of a bigger group of schools, linked together within a larger trust. Often these schools have head teachers who are, in turn, led by an executive head teacher with responsibility for all of the schools in the trust. Typically, the whole group will have the same pay and conditions.

Free schools

Free schools can be set up by anyone who meets the requirements in an application process set out by the government. This means they do not have to follow local authority policies and may have very different pay and conditions.

Faith schools

A pick 'n' mix all of their own! The most common faith schools are Roman Catholic (often named after a saint) and Church of England schools, but depending on your location, you may find others, such as Sikh and Islamic schools. These schools may have admission criteria linked to the associated faith but will not necessarily be exclusive. Again, ensure you check the pay and conditions policy.

Independent schools

As with state schools, there are a wide variety of independent schools. While the fact that parents, in most cases, have to pay fees may act as a natural filter, which could mean that you have fewer challenges with kids who have neither the inclination nor the aptitude to become great learners, you may also find a pressurised expectation to produce results, as paying parents expect a good return on their fees. However, as a teacher you will probably benefit from smaller classes and there are often very good facilities.

And there's more …

Within all of these different types of schools, there are also single sex schools. Boys' schools and girls' schools can be very different in how they 'feel', so make sure you are comfortable in that environment.

Every single school has its own ethos, individual environment and unique atmosphere. You can pick up some of this by visiting the school's website and looking at the latest Ofsted report. However, the teaching world is a small place and nothing beats a bit of insider information, so ask around and you will often find someone who can give you the inside line.

The next step is applying for a job …

Your shop window

Your letter of application is your shop window. It needs to be just like those fantastic displays that stop you in your tracks, make you walk a little closer and eventually step into the shop.

We're going to begin with a top tip here. The number one top tip, actually, when it comes to applying for a job.

TOP TIP

To get to first base you have to get on to the interview shortlist. To do so, you must make your application stand out.

We don't mean with coloured paper, pictures or flashy fonts; we mean you need to personalise it to each and every job. Don't be lazy. Don't think you can get away with one letter of application and just tweak it. These letters stand out a mile, usually because they contain mistakes. You might be surprised but we've had the following beauties over the years:

♦ The wrong school.

♦ The wrong job title.

♦ An application to a boys' school when it was mixed sex.

♦ An application to a primary when it was secondary!

♦ Best of all, this is the actual total content of a letter of application we received a few years ago: 'I would like to apply for the post of mathematics teacher. I do not intend to write any further on the topic as I am a great teacher and you should give me the job.' This application was quickly stored in the nearest cylindrical filing cabinet! You can be a little too assertive.

When you apply for a teaching job, there is typically one main document – the application form. This will usually ask you to complete a section (with the option of extra sheets) explaining how you meet the person specification. It is increasingly likely, due to 'safer recruitment' practices, that you will not be asked for a CV, so we would only recommend sending one if it is specifically requested.

The person specification needs to be treated carefully. Craft your statement so you clearly signpost how your skills and experiences meet the criteria. Often, the advertisement will indicate which skills are 'essential' and 'desirable', so systematically work through the list. Ensure that you cover them all and make it easy for those doing the shortlisting to spot your potential.

Then add the 'So what?' factor.

> I have great experience of using computer software such as Microsoft Word and PowerPoint.

So what? What does this actually tell your potential employer? You can use a PC. Well, so can all graduates. Tell them *what* you have done with students on your teaching practices and, even more importantly, what the outcomes were.

> I am really passionate about physical education.

Zzzzzzzzzzzzzzzzzzzzzzzzzzzzzzzzzzzzzzzzzzzzzzzzzzzzzzz! You wouldn't believe how many subjects we've heard about someone's passion for (ooh er, missus!).

What we want to hear about is *why* you are passionate and what your passion will do for the students at our school. We want to know what *you* will bring to the table and what you have done before that illustrates it.

So, for every one of the skills and attributes you cover, build in the 'So what?' factor. For example:

> During my teaching practice I introduced 2D design software within a differentiated project to a Year 8 mixed ability group and, using this, each

student was able to use a laser-cutter success-fully for the first time to produce a high quality 3D product.

TOP TIPS

FIVE LITTLE EXTRAS THAT WILL GIVE YOU BONUS POINTS

- ◆ Mention what you will do as extra-curricular activities – that extra factor that you will bring to the school.

- ◆ If you are a specialist, mention any other subjects you can comfortably teach. Schools like flexibility.

- ◆ If you don't know the name of the head teacher, find out and address the application to him or her.

- ◆ Add something that shows you have a sense of humour (preferably not your favourite 'knock knock' joke or that picture of your best mate on a night out!).

- ◆ Say something about pastoral care or how you might fit in there (there's plenty about this area later on).

A foot in the door

Hopefully, all this great preparation will have offers of interviews flying your way. You are in with a shout of your first teaching job so you need to get your interview head on.

Your first task is to read what is required of you on the day. Not just the time and place but also what you need to take with you. This usually includes your proof of ID (a passport is best but photo ID otherwise), criminal record check (currently called the Disclosure and Barring Service), and degree certificate. You may also be asked for other things, such as samples of your work with students, your own work (if it's a practical subject), a presentation, lesson plans and so on. The key, as before, is getting your best Scout thinking going and being prepared. We have personal experience of at least three people arriving for an interview and being turned away because they couldn't prove who they were. This is all about safeguarding; your training course should have briefed you fully on this so it is something you should be sharp on. We will cover this briefly in Chapter 3, but you can expand your knowledge on the internet or via a friendly teacher.

What to wear

Does this actually matter? Too right it does. Depending on the school you are being interviewed for, it can matter a lot. The different types of school we described earlier will all have different expectations for student and staff dress. There may be a strict uniform for pupils, a non-uniform policy or something in-between. Some schools have a staff dress code (you can find this out from the website or by asking your spies); others just expect staff to dress professionally. The latter actually means that the staff wear clothing that is in harmony with the student dress policy so as to not undermine it.

TOP TIPS

FOR INTERVIEW DRESSING

♦ Look smart, think smart – no matter what type of school.

♦ Fellas: wear a tie and do up your top button.

♦ Don't wear anything that makes you stand out vividly.

♦ Polish your shoes and, if you buy new ones, take the stickers off the soles!

♦ Iron shirts, tops and blouses.

On that last subject, this is what happened to Gary during an interview for a headship. At the end of the first day, the school governors decided it would be a good plan to take all the candidates to a hotel overnight in order to take them out of their comfort zone (as if six interview panels hadn't already managed that!). The field had already been cut from eight to three candidates and, after a meal with governors, other local head teachers and representatives from the local authority, it was off to bed.

Each candidate was given a time to report to a particular room in the morning. Gary got up, ate breakfast, dressed casually to avoid any disasters with jam or brown sauce, then nipped back to his room, popped on his new light grey suit and, having decided he looked the part, headed for the interview room.

Once there, he was given a topic for a presentation and told to return in ten minutes to impress the interview panel. Gary, now feeling the pressure of the extra cup of tea he had slurped at breakfast, decided to zip back to his room and use the loo. Now, we know what you're thinking! But you're wrong; he managed the toilet perfectly well. It was the water pressure on the spray-nozzle tap that caught him by surprise, splattering his light grey trousers better than a Jackson Pollack painting, simulating a badly directed wee event! Thinking quickly, Gary found the room's hairdryer and blasted his trousers to desert-like dryness then looked at his watch. One minute left!

So, the last top tip on interview dress is *wear dark trousers*!

Gary got the job, though, after blitzing the presentation with no preparation. Apparently adrenaline is a useful interview aid, but we wouldn't recommend you rely on it.

First impressions

Back to the interview. You are suited and booted and ready to go. Do you know what time you need to set off? How far is it? Do your research, even do a dry run if needs be. Just don't turn up late, unless there is a pile-up on the motorway.

It is likely that you will meet the head teacher or a senior member of staff early on. So, the first job is to get your body language right. By this we mean smile and look them in the eye while introducing yourself and telling them you are pleased to meet them. Sounds simple, you wouldn't believe how many candidates make no eye contact or mumble something unintelligible. Given that you are applying for a job as a communicator, this is your first test. The second is your handshake. What's yours like? Please tell us it's not one of those flimsy tips of the finger jobs. If you want to show you are confident, shake hands confidently and grasp their hand properly.

Miss greeted her · NEW · head in the same way she'd been greeting children for years...

By now you will have begun to get a feel of the school and the people who work there. If you are like us, when we arrived for our respective interviews at the same school, we picked up the vibe straight away that we would feel comfortable there and wanted to be part of it. Equally, we have both picked up vibes in other places that set alarm bells ringing. Unless you think you are in the last chance saloon, don't be afraid to withdraw from an interview. The process is as much about your liking them, as it is them wanting you.

Interviews come in a variety of shapes and sizes, with all sorts of tasks to test your abilities. These are the most likely plot-lines for the day.

Tour of the school

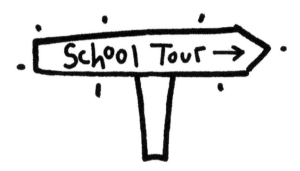

Every aspect of the selection day is part of your interview. Don't think that the 'informal' tour, often led by the head teacher or another senior member of staff, is not part of the process of sussing you out. What you do and what you say is all taken in, and even if you find yourself in the company of student tour guides, it's probable that they will give feedback on the tour, as will anyone else you meet.

TOPTiPS

FOR SCHOOL TOURS

♦ Talk to staff and students if you stop in classrooms. Show you are child centred and interested in what they are learning.

♦ Ask your guide two or three focused questions (you can prepare for this).

♦ Avoid hogging the tour guide and getting pally. Get into a Tour de France frame of mind: stick in the main peloton, make a break for the front, then drop back to catch a breather. You can repeat this strategically as you move around.

Out and about

You may well have some free time during the day. Make use of it, but remember you are still on show. Walls have eyes and ears! Try to talk to some key people – as many in your prospective department as you can. Aim to ask pertinent questions while dropping in snippets of information about your skills and experiences.

Here is a cracking example of how not to do it. Sometime ago we had a big interview going on at our school. The candidates all arrived at reception and after a short wait were whisked off to formally start the day. Or so they thought. The day, in fact, had already started, as those candidates were on show as soon as they walked in – reception staff, after all, form judgements and often pass them on. Initially, it was so far so good. However, a little later, one candidate returned to reception when he had some 'free time' and asked, 'Where is the stunningly beautiful one who was here earlier?' No prizes for those spotting the fatal error and imagining the disgruntlement of the other 'less beautiful' receptionists! Oddly enough, he didn't stay for the full interview and was 'cut' early.

Never underestimate the power of staff in a school. Everyone will give feedback, especially if they see you negatively, so take heed. Receptionists are sharp as racing snakes and could be given the job title, Director of First Impressions. Don't say we didn't warn you!

Student council interview

A few years ago, some members of the press got student council interviews wrong, believing that students were making decisions about who was offered a teaching job. In reality, student interviews are used to gauge how well a candidate interacts with young people. There will typically be an 'observer' present who is watching and listening to your every move.

TOP TIPS

FOR STUDENT INTERVIEWS

◆ Engage your audience as you would a class. Answer closed questions as if they were open questions, giving full and interesting answers.

◆ Be a teacher not a friend. Talk in a friendly manner, of course, but don't overdo it.

◆ Talk to the students, not the observer.

◆ Ask some questions back as part of your answers. You can incorporate this into your fact finding about the school.

- ♦ This is a great opportunity to bring up any extra-curricular clubs you might run. You can make a statement here on how much time you will give to them.

- ♦ Avoid controversial or unseemly topics, unless asked. We had a candidate once who talked about their passion for hunting with crossbows. Unsurprisingly, it scared the kids!

Meet the department

A visit to the department is your chance to sell yourself to your future colleagues. You need to meet them all, so strategically tick them off in your head or prepare early and have a notebook with you listing names and questions. You can ask about schemes of work, setting policies, support, marking, continuing professional development, resources and so on, but if you are super-clever, you can frame your questions in such a way that it allows you to drop in something about your own strengths.

Teach a lesson

Depending on the number of candidates and the timings of the day, you are likely to have a shorter amount of time than a typical lesson to teach a class. Usually you will have been given a topic and told something about the class. By all means, if there is anything you are not sure of before you arrive, ask for clarification, but don't mither the life out of the school asking for reading and spelling ages, national curriculum levels, IQ scores and all manner of things about the students, like a recent candidate did with us. Alarm bells rang!

TOP TIPS

FOUR KEY THINGS THE SCHOOL WANTS TO FIND OUT ABOUT YOU

- Can you plan a lesson? (Take a plan to give your observer.)
- Can you command and engage the class? (Welcome the kids energetically and introduce yourself before getting on with the show.)
- Can you manage a classroom?
- Can you challenge the kids and get them learning stuff?

Interview with curriculum leader

The aim of the selection game is to find out what you know – that is, whether you have got the subject knowledge and skills to be worth employing. The key here is to be honest. Say what you can do and give examples with outcomes, but if you have gaps, say so and link it to the sort of professional development you would like to pursue in future. No candidate will have all of the cards in the pack, and those who say they do are usually the jokers!

This is another opportunity to talk about the extras you will bring, so ask a few questions to illustrate your sharpness. Again, plan ahead.

Final interview

Some schools cut the field at a certain point, others may not. If you get to the final stage you are in with a shout, but be certain that you want the job and can deliver before you go on. If you are offered the job you will be expected to say yes.

Enter the room with a decent handshake for all present (and leave with another, thanking the panel for the opportunity). Expect to have up to four people present, although it may be fewer. Whatever the situation, remember to address your answers to the gallery and not just to the person who asked the question.

With all of your answers, you need to engage your audience and embroider your answers with examples and outcomes. The likely themes will be:

♦ Safeguarding

♦ Teaching strategies

♦ Pastoral care

♦ Assessment

♦ Student management and engagement

After the questions are over, this is your last chance to shine. Ask a question of your own and try to link it cunningly to something that you want them to know about you – and not just that you want the job.

It's common practice for schools to make a decision on the day and let you know while you are in the school – some even have the contract ready for signing before you leave. Alternatively, they may telephone you later.

If you are successful, crack open a bottle of wine or a box of chocolates (or both!). If not, aim to bounce back quickly. Remember to ask for feedback – if it is given honestly, it can be invaluable for the next interview.

Chapter 2

FIRST STEPS

Congratulations, you got the job! If you have come through the conventional route of school and university into teaching, then you have just jumped your first hurdle: getting a job. That is scary stuff. Up until this point in your life, you didn't have a lot to think about. We know it probably didn't feel like that at the time, when you were sweating your way through SATs, GCSEs, A levels, finals and all that, but look back now and you will see that basically all you had to do was get up, go to whichever establishment you were attached to at the time, do what you were told and come home. Suddenly the drawbridge is pulled up on all that, and you've got to find someone who is going to pay you enough to finance your extensive social life. That means you've got to enter a competition (called applying for a job) and you've got to come first. The days of 'Well done!', 'Top effort today!' and 'You can be proud of yourself for coming second!' are over. Second isn't good enough.

But you came first! This will be one of the best feelings you will ever have. Somebody wants you. It's like falling in love with someone who wants to fall in love with you. Well, almost. You will be overwhelmed with feelings of pride (you have known for ages how wonderful you are, but now it is official – someone else called your employer thinks so too), but there will be other emotions as well, such as relief. Everyone has read the horror stories about spending three or four years getting yourself qualified up to your eyeballs and then there is no job at the end of it.

Having given yourself this statutory ego boost, just look at it from your employer's perspective for a moment. When someone leaves a school the words on everyone's lips are, 'It won't be the same without you.' Usually this is for all the right reasons, namely that a valued member of the school community is leaving a void which will impoverish school life for ever. Occasionally, of course, there will be an institutional sigh of relief, but we will leave that for another day. (Gary recalls in his first school that the collection for the leaving present of a less than fully respected colleague contained several paperclips.) The fact is that the school leadership team will probably have thought, 'He or she will be hard to replace.' You will soon see that this book is based on an inestimable pride in teachers and a belief that almost all teachers are incredible magicians who perform daily miracles because of their huge arsenal of skills and indefatigable work ethic.

What is the solution to this gaping hole left by your predecessor? You! Job descriptions have been drawn up, advertisements published, applications received, interviews conducted and you have been appointed. What you will not realise is how nervous school leaders can be on the day of the interview. They want to appoint someone who will be fantastic for their school, and guess what, they have chosen you. You were the best person there, and you have beaten all the opposition. No doubt you are eternally grateful to them for offering you employment. But they, in turn, are immensely grateful that you have come along. There is a job that needs doing and you have been judged the best person to do it. Be proud of yourself and enjoy every single moment.

Before you start, you will almost certainly have the opportunity to visit the school, so our next task is to give you some advice and guidance on how to go about this first visit.

We're not going to bang on about this, but the same applies to working in a school as it does for interviews: get your clothing and appearance right. You may think you have seen enough of your future colleagues to judge this accurately, but think twice before you turn up with your new pink hair and lederhosen.

There will be various forms to fill in on this first visit, most importantly your bank details so you can be paid. Find out in advance what the school might need to see in terms of identification. It is likely to be photo ID and confirmation of your address, plus any professional documentation. You may or may not have received your certificates from your training institution, but if you've got them, bring them along.

TOP TIP

Rule of thumb number one: make sure you have understood where you have to be, at what time and who you are meeting.

Teachers are busy folk – you will find that out in due course – so there is nothing more irritating than having agreed a set time to meet and greet your new colleague, only to find they are late or have misunderstood the arrangements. Schools can be big places, often with several different buildings, so make sure you are clear about where exactly you have to report and at what time. Unbelievably, a young colleague fell foul of her initial teacher training tutor because they had said, 'We'll see you at 8.30 a.m. on Tuesday. I'm teaching first lesson, so we can have some time together during lesson 2.' This was interpreted as 'There's no point in coming in before lesson 2'. Result? A young and nervous NQT getting off on the wrong foot.

Obviously, the worst can happen. Washing machines leak at the most inappropriate times and other people can be terribly selfish in wanting to use the roads at the same time as you, rendering the sat nav prediction of the time required to get from home to school well short of the time it actually takes. If you are delayed, contact the school and let them know. It's a simple courtesy.

What do you want to achieve on this first visit? First and foremost, try not to be overwhelmed. You can expect people to be pleased to see you. After the interview, all involved will want to know who was appointed. Names will not mean much, but staff will say things like, 'The tall one with glasses', so you will be recognised and people will almost certainly be very welcoming and genuinely pleased to see you. Enjoy it!

The children may have different approaches. If you are going into a secondary school, beware. The big ones will look awfully big; some may even have beards (mostly the boys!). There is often a weird and unquantifiable illusion at work at these times. When Chris used to coach cricket teams everybody else's players always seemed to look bigger. The oldest students always look huge when you don't know them. We think this might be a law of quantum physics but, we promise, they shrink with familiarity. As you get established, and you start to get some years under your belt, you will tend to associate students with how big they were when you first knew them, so they are always the size of an 11-year-old in your mind. In the meantime, don't be shocked or intimidated by their size. They are only kids; big kids, yes, but kids nonetheless!

TOP TIP

If a student is substantially bigger than you and you need to have a firm word with them, sit down. This minimises any feeling of physical inadequacy you might have. It's hard to overcome the disadvantage you may feel in having a conversation with a student when you can only look up their nose!

In a primary school, you will find yourself surrounded by ankle grabbers. The littlies may be lovely, but as you will know from your training, they love to tug on your shirt tails to tell you something incredibly important, like their dog's name or that it's their birthday next week. It's just a matter of getting used to the differences and having strategies to cope.

The children will adopt different ways of having a first look at you. Most of them will be quietly welcoming, watching you intently so they can start to get the measure of you. The secret to this is body language. You may well be feeling nervous, with a few butterflies inside, but don't let that show. Use your eyes and establish confident eye contact.

TOP TiP

Your eyes are your most potent weapons. An inability to maintain eye contact is an immediate giveaway and children will pick this up straight-away.

Look into my eyes...

Children are extraordinarily loyal, but they are not ready to be loyal to you yet. They hardly know you. They will be waiting and watching. They may even be apparently devoted to their previous teacher, and you may find this personally hurtful. Be patient – your turn will come. They will need a solid bedrock and sound relationships before they are ready to transfer their loyalty to you, but it will happen. It is a bit like when a much treasured family pet ascends the great escalator in the sky. It takes a while to take a new incumbent to your heart, but once it starts to happen, it can happen very quickly.

Consequently, don't throw yourself at them like a court jester; keep your shots in your locker for now. Be friendly, err on the side of being matter of fact, transmit to them that you are looking forward to being their teacher and drop in a couple of pieces of choice information which they can relate to. A primary school NQT opened a rich seam with her class-to-be when one of them saw she had a scar on her elbow. This elicited a story about how her older brother had pushed her off her bicycle when she was 6, and stories of similar scars and comparable calamities ensued. A gentle bond was formed, and there was the start of her 'discipline' (we'll return to this in Chapter 4).

You will probably be shadowing another teacher on this first visit. Watch how that teacher interacts with the children and other staff members. It's all about relationships. (Remember that 'decisive element' quote from the Introduction?)

TOP TIPS

FOR YOUR FIRST VISIT

- ◆ How does each lesson start? What are the conventions for calling the class to order?

- ◆ How does the teacher deal with latecomers? How do they manage questioning, including that most precious of skills, dealing with a child who has offered a wrong answer?

- How do they get the reluctant on board? How do they deal with the early finishers?

- How do they use questioning techniques to probe and develop the understanding of the more capable learners?

- How do they deal with the chair-swingers, the ones who turn around, the ones who talk when the teacher is talking, the ones who are in dreamland?

Your antennae should be working overtime, looking and learning to pick up examples of good practice. One of the benefits of our great profession is that, when observing others, you can continually cherry-pick. Many is the time when you watch someone else and think, 'That was good but it wouldn't work for me' or 'It wouldn't work with my class on a Thursday afternoon when they can be tricky.' In fact, you have an excellent automatic triage system in your brain which sorts out what will work for you and discards what won't.

During this first visit you should be provided with some key information. First, you should be given your timetable so that you know what you are teaching, to whom and when. Obviously, the range of possibilities are more limited in a primary school, but even there it will be important for you to know where they go on a Wednesday morning for music, what time they return from swimming on a Friday and how the joint session for PE works on a Monday.

Second, once you've got your timetable, do a 'timetable walk' so that you know, geographically, where you need to be for each lesson, including tutor time and assemblies, where appropriate.

Third, you will need to know the timings of the day. How long are lessons? When is breaktime? Lunchtime? What are the arrangements for the end of the day, especially for primary schools?

Fourth, you need to know what you are going to be teaching. This should take two forms: the programme for the term or year (including any assessment dates) and what you should be covering on the first day. This will give you an overall picture of where your lesson fits into the grand scheme of things and, more potently, you will also know what you will be doing on the first morning.

Fifth, you will need a list of names for each class.

TOP TIP

Look down the list of names and immediately spot any which may be hazardous to pronounce.

Some names can be tricky to pronounce because of the ethnic background of the family or it may just be an unusual name. But there is nothing worse than being derailed on that very first register call by you mispronounceating a name, which will result in sniggers all round at your expense. It is also worth asking the existing teacher if there are any variations or shortened forms of names that you should know. The register may say Andrew but only his parents call him Andrew, everyone else calls him Andy. This information can be priceless. If you can get these things right, you will start to build your relationships with the students on the firm ground from which that magic loyalty is fashioned; if you get it wrong, it can be disastrous for you and your self-esteem on that first nervous morning.

Failing this, if you get to the first morning and are not confident that you have done your preparation as thoroughly as you would like, there is nothing wrong with saying to the class, 'I have looked at your names and I am going to learn them as soon as possible. Is there anyone who likes to be called by a different name to what I have in my register? Andrew, do you like being called Andrew or Andy?' Do not hesitate to say to the children something like, 'You have a brilliant name but I have never come across it before. Can you give me some help in saying it properly?' This will impress them immediately, sending a signal that each one of them matters to you and that you want to get things right. Make it sound as though it is your fault for not knowing how to say their name, rather than theirs for having an unusual name.

Finally, once you have got the basic roll call of names, you need as much preliminary information as possible to help you on day one. This will cover any inside information such as special educational needs, medical conditions or behavioural issues. Detailed data can probably come later, but there will be certain salient pieces of information that you will need to know, so make sure you ask. For example, you might ask if any of your students are 'looked after' or have free school meals, as you may well want to track their progress very carefully. This will impress your host teacher and will send the message that you are a sharp act.

While you are in school, use this opportunity to get some of the basic geography of the place under your belt. You will not accomplish this all in one go, even in a small primary school. There will be cupboards and store areas which will not offer up their secrets to you for many a while yet! But certain things are a must:

♦ Staff toilets (enough said)

♦ Staffroom/workroom

♦ Anywhere where you teach

♦ Where assemblies are held

♦ Caretaker's office (stuff will need fixing and sorting)

♦ ICT technician's den

♦ Medical room/area (Where do you send sick kids?)

Find out what the arrangements are for breaktime and lunchtime. Does everyone bring their own tea or coffee? Is there a 'staff fund' to which everyone donates to pay for milk/tea/coffee in the staffroom?

There will be other conventions to take on board as well. How should you address the head? It could be by their first name, it could be Mr/Mrs … or it could be by their initials (yes, some schools have a strange habit of using people's initials). It can be extremely embarrassing to get this wrong, and the same applies to all senior members of staff and, indeed, all your colleagues. If in doubt, err on the side of formality, and that means Mr/Mrs …

How do the children address members of staff? Usually it is Sir or Miss, sometimes accompanied by a surname, although it is not unknown for older students to use first names. It is essential to find out. If you stand in front of a class in a 'traditional' school and invite the children to call you Deirdre, you could be in for a rough ride. (Nothing wrong with being called Deirdre, by the way – well, not much, unless you are actually called Alan!)

Also look out for practices which affect how the children behave. At the beginning of each session or lesson, do they line up outside? Do they stand behind their chairs? Do they say 'Good morning'? What happens at the end of the lesson? Are they expected to put chairs away tidily at the end of every lesson? At the end of the day, do they put the chairs on the desks? What about uniform? Are they allowed to wear make-up or jewellery? What about boys' ties? Can they be worn half-mast or is there is an expectation that they are knotted properly? What about shirts? Do they have to be tucked in?

It is crucial for you to get these things right, so the quicker you pick up which way the wind blows, the better. You do not want an embarrassing conversation with a zealous deputy head who respectfully comes to point out on your second day that three members of your class are wearing make-up or are not wearing school uniform shoes; equally, you do not want to take issue with a child for wearing trainers if actually trainers are okay. As the old saying goes, get the little things right, and the big things will take care of themselves.

If your head is not already spinning because there is so much to take in on this first visit, find out about what the form is for doing displays in the classrooms you will be using. If you are a secondary teacher, you may well be sharing your classroom with other staff; if you are a primary teacher, you might be lucky enough to have one room or area which will be 'yours'. Primary teachers often seem to be genetically more gifted at doing displays than their secondary colleagues (those dangling discs depicting the planets which decapitate any visiting adult over 5 foot 6 seem to be a necessary feature of every primary classroom). Before the start of the new term, you will want to spend time in the school during the holidays organising your room. This will not happen by magic, so find out what you can do and can't do. Where will you find backing paper, staples and so on? What can be thrown out and what can't?

Now, what we have said there may sound a bit odd – go in during the holidays? Can you imagine your bank manager or doctor doing that? We mention this simply because we think that if you want to be a super-teacher, it's worth investing a bit of the thirteen weeks a year you have designated as holiday into your career and your kids. Most brilliant teachers do this.

Finally, a little bit of self-help. Unions. *Join one!* In a career like teaching, you never know what is round the corner, however diligent you are, so you must protect yourself. All manner of different scenarios can ambush you and sometimes they can be threatening. Being in a union gives you guidance and support. Each union stands for something different, so research carefully into what they each represent and choose the one which suits you best, especially if there is industrial action in the air. It is very important that you are comfortable with the organisation you are joining. If it's only legal protection you are after, and don't want the political side, then there are schemes like that out there too. You should find information in your new staffroom and on the internet.

TOP TIP

Join a union – you never know what is round the corner.

You have now taken the first steps on your journey in this wonderful and exciting profession of ours. When you get home, treat yourself to something nice, in a glass maybe. You can even put wine in it. It's worth celebrating. You will already have been hit by a welter of information; you now need to digest it and sort it into some sort of reasonable order.

Your career beckons. Have a great time!

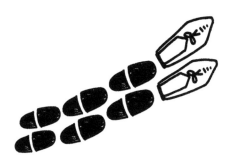

flying Solo

Chapter 3

FIRST FEW DAYS
FROM TRAINING DAYS TO FLYING SOLO

You have arrived. You have made it. This is the day you have dreamed of – your first day flying solo. The day you arrive in your new school for the beginning of term will be completely different to your visit to the school in preparation for this momentous day. You will no longer be wearing an ID badge which says 'Visitor'. As soon as the admin team can get you photographed, you will have a badge which bears your name. Having been known by your first name or even a nickname all the way through university, now you are Mr, Mrs or Miss …. You have arrived. You have grown up.

There will be other potent reminders that you are now a fully signed up member of staff. You will have a pigeon hole in the staffroom. Yes, indeed, the world is truly now your footstool! Don't be misled into thinking that this is an unreservedly good thing – it also means all manner of people can now communicate with you and expect you to do things – but let us enjoy the moment for now. It signifies status.

The boost to your nervous ego will not stop there. You will almost certainly be entrusted with keys. These may enable entry and security to your own room or, if you are extra privileged, you may be given a master key which enables you to gain access to anywhere in the building. Yes, folks, this is proper responsibility!

In the course of the day, you should be provided with access codes, passwords and usernames for the school computer systems, which will open up yet further corridors of investigation. And if you want one more indicator that you have finally arrived, have a quick look at a timetable. Before today, your predecessor's initials will have been emblazoned on the timetable against your classes. Even worse, it may have said something along the lines of 'AN Other Maths Teacher' as the exciting news of your appointment was awaited. Now it will bear your initials. There is absolutely no doubt – you are a proper teacher at last.

We are going to divert for one moment to offer a wider homily on an NQT's feelings on this first day of term. It would be perfectly normal and expected for you to feel excited, nervous, proud, daunted … a whole cocktail of different emotions. A true teacher looks forward to the beginning of every term and every school year.

TOP TIP

If ever you find yourself dreading the beginning of term, jump ship. You are doing the wrong thing with your life, and you are not doing yourself or the children any favours. It may be the wrong school or the wrong career, but it's a decision that has to be made.

Yes, yes, yes, when the alarm goes off on that first morning at some ungodly hour, which you haven't seen for six or more weeks, dragging yourself from the warmth of your duvet and the comfort of Morpheus can seem less than desirable, but once you are up and running you should be anticipating with relish the chance to meet new children. Your creative juices should be flowing on how to engage your pupils with the content and skills you love. You should be considering the possibilities for this year's school play or a school trip in the summer. The school calendar is a kaleidoscope of activity with its own rhythm and milestones: Harvest Festival becomes Halloween becomes Diwali becomes Remembrance becomes Christmas, and so it goes on. As teachers, this offers us a priceless opportunity to influence and change lives.

In all probability, you will start with an INSET or training day. This is a huge bonus! You will almost certainly take some stick from friends who are not teachers throughout your career about long holidays, finishing at 3 p.m.

and training days. Get used to it. Smile! Ask them why they aren't teachers if they think it's so cushy. Invite them to shadow you for a day. Usually they will say, 'Oh, I couldn't be a teacher! I would throttle them before breaktime!' Game, set and match to you. The favourite jibe is, 'You've just had six weeks' holiday. Why don't you have the training days in the holiday?' The answer is, 'We do. The five training days are in addition to the 195 days of term time when we deliver lessons.'

Make good use of the training day. But beware: it is no easy ride and you will go home with your head spinning. Nonetheless, it is a great way to find your feet for a day before the children arrive. You will almost certainly have a series of meetings, which will be quite intimidating for you because everyone else will seem to know what they are doing and you will be feeling very green. Don't be deceived. It's just an illusion that they all know what they are doing. And don't feel you have to be life and soul of the party – just soak up as much as you possibly can. You will never remember all of it, but you will know a thousand times more at the end of the day than you did when you arrived nervously at 8 a.m.

So, down to practicalities. On your preliminary visit in the term before you took up your post you should have come away with your timetable, the timings of the school day, your class lists and supplementary information about key children in your class, an idea of what you will be teaching first and how it fits into the overall scheme of learning. You are going to be feverishly busy in the first few days of term, so you will have been very wise if you have prepared your first series of lessons before the training day. It will be a massive plus for you to have those first lessons, plus the resources you need, in your locker before hostilities begin.

TOP TiPS

FOR WHAT TO FIND OUT ON TRAINING DAY

♦ Do you have to do a playground duty? When? Where? What exactly is expected? What about after school? Do you have to do a bus duty? What about lunchtime? In most schools you are not obliged to do lunchtime duties, but there may be a scheme to pay staff who volunteer. Find out!

♦ When do teachers have meetings? Dates? How long do they last? Where? Are there meetings before school? Which days?

♦ When are assemblies? How do they work? What are the expectations?

♦ Where are resources kept? How do you get photocopies done? Where will you find exercise books, folders, paper and other stationery?

♦ What are the requirements for marking?

- ◆ Who is your ITT tutor during your NQT year? What will your training involve? When will you have meetings? When will you be observed? What records do you need to keep? How will you use the ten per cent extra time that you will be granted on the timetable?

- ◆ What should you do if you are ill? Who should you ring? When?

- ◆ What should you do if you need to leave the premises during the school day? What is the system for signing out? What are your contracted times?

You may not find definitive answers to all of these questions immediately, but these issues should be on your tick list, starting with training day.

There are two other areas which you also need to start to familiarise yourself with: school rules and sanctions. There should be a staff handbook which will give you a comprehensive overview of the school rules. You probably won't have time on the training day to get your head around all of them, but you do need a synopsis. If in doubt, ask. In particular, you would benefit from knowing what is the expectation in terms of uniform, make-up and jewellery. What about coats and bags? What do the students do if it is wet before school, at breaktime or at lunchtime? What about mobile phones and other electronic devices?

Every school will have its own protocol on these matters, so ascertain what the regime is in your school. Also find out about the currency of rewards in the school. Are there systems of stickers, commendations, merits, texts home or gold stars? As we will explain in Chapter 5, praise is much more powerful than criticism if you want to achieve improved behaviour and effort. You need to find out how it works in your school.

Equally, you need to know how the sanctions system works. What should you do if you have a naughty child? What is the system for referring the child to a colleague, head of department or senior member of staff? What paper trails are involved? Are they done on a central-ised computer system or in paper form? What about detentions? At breaktime? At lunchtime? After school? We will describe discipline in greater detail in Chapter 4. At the moment, we are dealing with the first few days. You just need to know what basic structures and strate-gies are in place.

Then there's you! You are the most important person in all of this. Forget being terribly magnanimous for a moment, we are going to talk about *you*. The most important obligation every employer has is to ensure that you are safe in your place of employment. You should receive a full induction into the school's safe-guarding procedures. These are designed to guarantee the safety of employees and children alike. They are absolutely essential, and they cover some murky aspects of human behaviour. But as is highlighted all too often in the media, when these things go wrong, the effects on young people can be catastrophic.

TOP TIP

Safeguarding is a vital issue. Always pass on a disclosure from a child to the relevant individual.

Safeguarding should be taken extremely seriously and you should be given an in-depth introduction right at the beginning of your time at the school, often on a training day. You should then be aware of the possible dangers and also of what to do if you are confronted by a situation which has made your antennae quiver in the knowledge that something is wrong, either with a child or a colleague. The key thing to bear in mind is that under no circumstances do you keep a secret. If a child tells you something that is clearly of concern, you *must* pass it on, no matter how much the child begs you not to. It is in the child's best interest and also your own. There will be a designated individual in your school in charge of safeguarding and it is to that person you should turn if you receive a disclosure.

Make sure you know the procedures for a fire evacuation. Where is the nearest exit door to where you teach? Where is the closest fire assembly point? What happens at breaktime or lunchtime? What are you expected to do? As part of the school's security system there may be security codes on doors. You may need to know how to access these rooms so ask someone to give you the code.

Social media forums are here to stay. Being able to communicate with our friends and family instantly in a variety of ways is a part of modern life. But beware! You are now a professional person, so be very wary about what you put out there for public consumption. What may have been very amusing on holiday in the summer or at the rugby club at the weekend doesn't look so clever if your employer or the children you teach come across it. You now need to be extremely discreet about what is out there. If in doubt, don't!

Furthermore, you should also keep your professional life away from the social media – we know of schools where people have lost their jobs because of imprudent comments. If you engage in dialogue about school matters in open forums, you are likely to receive a very serious reprimand from your head teacher and governors. What happens in school stays in school; what happens in your private life is private. Keep it that way. Under no circumstances enter into communication with children on social media sites. If you want them to email their homework to you, they can do this using your school email address or virtual learning environment. Nothing else!

TOP TIP

What happens in school stays in school; what happens in your private life is private.

By the end of the training day, you should have your lesson plan folder set up and ready to go. You may be asked to follow a particular format by your curriculum leader or initial teacher training coordinator. This will vary from school to school, but whether the format is prescribed or if you have freedom to design your own, make sure it is fit for purpose. These next few weeks are going to be tough as you confront the twin demands of preparing the next lessons and marking work from the previous ones, as well as evaluating the lessons you have taught that day. You need a robust system and strict self-discipline; once you get behind, it becomes twice as hard to catch up.

The last challenge for this first foray into the life of your new school is to start to learn the names of other staff members. This can be quite daunting in a large secondary school, but give yourself a target of a few each day, starting with those you are going to be working with most closely.

Finally, enjoy the day and don't miss any early chances to join in. You want to get noticed, for all the right reasons, of course. Look keen, look smart and if an opportunity presents itself to volunteer for something you would like to do, quietly put your name forward. So, here is a challenge: how quickly can you volunteer for a trip, club or other extra-curricular activity, such as the school show? There is no need to be pushy, just keen as mustard.

You will be exhausted at the end of your training day. Yes, teaching is a fascinating and endlessly rewarding job, but it is also very demanding. Welcome to our world!

TOP TIP

A word of warning: you are going to be shattered at the end of this first week.

Fatigue is another issue your friends who are not teachers won't get. 'You can't be shattered,' they will cry, 'you've just had six weeks' holiday!' Yes, but they have not gone from the sleepy somnolence of holiday time to high-octane, outside-lane-of-the-motorway type activity, accelerating from 0 to 60 in a millisecond, while simultaneously juggling lesson planning and Kierra's fallout with Chelsee, which teachers do every day. You will be worn out because you have worked very long hours, you will have been giving your all for at least five hours a day, end to end, and you will feel as though you are losing your voice because your vocal chords are not used to being forced to project over such an extended period of time. On top of that, you will have met a whole new bunch of people, planned many lessons, marked many books, attended meetings and kept a series of other metaphorical plates spinning. Be consoled

that you are not unusual in feeling absolutely flaked out at the end of the first week. If you are, you are doing everything right!

As the children arrive back at school, fresh faced and bright eyed for their new term, they will spot you immediately. You are new, so they will want to know who you are and where you are at. They will make two essential demands of you before they start to give you that most precious gift, their loyalty. You have got to earn it by meeting their two fundamental demands. First, that you teach them something. Yes, they do, in a rather traditional and old-fashioned way, expect to learn something when they come to school. Second, that you control them. And be under no illusion – they will test you out on this one to see what you are made of.

It is, therefore, of fundamental importance from the word go that every subliminal message which is being transmitted onto their radar screen beams up the message: 'This is my jungle and I am Tarzan. I know what I am doing and we will do things *my* way. I am organised and I know exactly what I want, so you can learn as much as possible. You will be safe in my classroom and I will look after you.'

What does this look like in practice? Let's get one thing straight, you are their leader. You are not a facilitator or an enabler. You are there to lead them, and when you lead them well they will respect you and will do anything for you. In the course of this, they will learn a lot and be as successful as they can possibly be. Your displays will be neat, tidy and well-organised, incorporating material that is relevant to supporting their learning. You will need to spend time organising classroom displays during the holidays. All shelves, trays, drawers and surfaces need to be rigorously sorted. When each group of children arrive in your room, chairs need to be shipshape under the tables, curtains need to be arranged as you want them and any stray bits of paper or pencil sharpenings should be cleared from the floor. You should insist on this with military strictness, and do not feel that you should be doing this yourself every time. Use small battalions: get the previous group to leave everything tidy and have clear procedures for this.

TOP TIP

It is essential that you do a seating plan for every lesson, where appropriate.

Seating plans are probably the first big message that you will send to your new class that you want things done your way. They are absolutely fundamental. Do not fall into the trap of thinking, 'I will leave it a few lessons until I've got to know them a bit better.' Your chance has gone. Do it from day one. If you are challenged about this, you need to say something like, 'It will help me to get to know your names as quickly as possible.' This is a solid reason which they will understand. First, you need a 'map' of how the tables are configured. Do this on the training day or on your first visit to the school. Then get your class list and assign children to seats on your map. As you know very little about the students at this point, we suggest you go either alphabetical or boy/girl. This is entirely uncontroversial. If challenged along the lines of, 'Why have I got to sit next to …?', you have a ready answer.

Of course, it may become apparent to you very soon that you want to change things. Some pairings may be obviously unsuitable or you may want to group by ability on some tables. Fine, you can always rearrange.

Indeed, sometimes certain individuals are instructed not to sit next to each other. If they tell you that, trust them and tweak the plan temporarily. You may even want to say, 'This will be our seating plan until next Friday.' This gives you a time frame which they will understand and accept. Once you get to know them better, you will probably want to rearrange anyway. Think carefully about where you want to put the chair-swingers, the chatterboxes, the dreamers, the turn-arounders.

You will almost certainly want to divide and rule the more reluctant learners. Consider using a very compliant child to act as a buffer for a more challenging child. You may have the luxury of an empty seat which can be useful for those who have wall-to-wall difficulties with the human race. If challenged, do not duck the issue. Remember the first of those two fundamental demands: they expect you to control them, so don't shy away from looking them in the eye and telling them, 'I'm putting you there because you will work harder and you will learn more, which is brilliant.' Crucially, thank them once they have complied. This will show that you are in charge but also that you respect them; with older students, in particular, this can be invaluable.

Once the opening weeks are over, think about how often you want to change your seating plan. It can have a remarkably refreshing effect. Just sitting in a different part of the room, either near to the window or viewing the lesson from the other side of the room, or sitting next to someone new can give everyone a lift. As a general rule of thumb, challenge yourself to alter your seating plan, and possibly even the configuration of tables where that is possible, about twice a term. Children benefit from change, especially a change in who they sit next to. It could be a friend, then someone they don't normally sit with, a boy, then a girl, someone of similar ability, someone of different ability. Ring the changes!

TOP TIP

Change your seating plan when spirits start to flag in the long autumn term.

Aim to change your seating plan at the end of November, as this is the time in the autumn term when spirits flag. It has been a long time since the October break, and it is still a long time until the Christmas run-in. Everybody needs refreshing. Also make some changes to your classroom displays, tables – anything you can – because it will revitalise everyone and give you that lift to carry you into the Christmas period.

Before we move on from seating plans, let us touch on your most important task once the children arrive: to learn their names. Of course, a written seating plan will be invaluable to you. You will win immediate Brownie points if you are able to take a nonchalant glance at your seating plan before addressing a child in your new class by the correct name. Sometimes you will be challenged by a child who may say, 'How do you know my name?', so be ready to tell them that you want to help them to do really well at school, and you can't do that without knowing who they are. Remember also the advice in the last chapter about names with which you may be unfamiliar and names by which children might prefer to be called.

You will have an early decision to make about how you work best. You should aim to be in school at least half an hour before the bell in the morning to ensure that everything is in place for the day. Once it starts, you will go helter-skelter through to 3 p.m., so you need to be well-organised. At the end of the school day, you will probably need some time to let the adrenaline and the busyness of the day settle. Don't get so busy that you forget to have some refreshments at this stage of the day.

Tea + Cake

Make sure that everything in your room is ready for the next day, which will give you an early opportunity to make friends with a key player in the school: the cleaner. They can be your greatest ally! They will not only keep your room shining like a new pin, but they will notice the chair which is wobbly and report it to the caretaker, so that you don't have the embarrassment the next day of a child collapsing off a three-legged chair. They will spot the edging strip of the table which, if not mended, will certainly tear your clothing when you catch yourself on it. One of the battle scars that every teacher has is the bruise on your thigh caused by bumping into tables. You are busy and hardly notice it at the time, but in the shower you look at your war wounds and wonder where they came from!

Look after your cleaner and your caretaker and they will be there when you need them. It is well worth checking how they want the chairs arranged at the end of the day, and ensuring that the windows are closed and that lights and computers have been turned off before you leave; safe in the knowledge that when a child is sick in your room they will come quickly to your rescue. As soon as you arrive, start to build alliances with every member of the school team – secretaries, cleaners, caretakers, dinner staff. They will all at some stage be invaluable to you.

You now have a decision to make. Are you better off staying in school and doing all the marking and preparation you need to do or will you work better at home? There is no single answer to this question. It depends on you and on your personal circumstances, but you need to establish a clear working pattern to your week and your weekends. The friends who like to tease you mercilessly about long holidays and finishing at 3 p.m. won't get this, but you will have to do a lot of work at weekends and at home, especially in the early stages.

How are you going to manage this? Many teachers like to make Friday evenings and Saturdays school-free zones. They then apply themselves to school work again on Sunday, but it is up to you to establish your own working routine. This is all about a healthy work–life balance. There are no shortcuts. You have joined a profession which demands a massive amount of you. Yes, you do get those long holidays, but if you work as hard as you need to in order to be a really good teacher, you will deserve them!

At the end of your first day of teaching, sit back and reflect. Yes, you will have faced some challenges but you will have also done lots of good things. Focus on the positive stuff. Then repeat this exercise once you have reached the end of your first full week, but this time crack open a bottle or a box of chocolates and celebrate your progress. You will have made mistakes, but you will have already progressed in your teaching and, importantly, begun to change young lives for the good.

Your final bit of reflection now needs to focus on those things you might like to work on improving next. Discuss them with your mentor, your head of department or curriculum leader. What matters is that, now you have arrived, you learn to look forward and you always regard yourself as being a learner in the classroom too.

Chapter 4

DISCIPLINE

The D word. Discipline is probably every teacher's greatest concern at the outset of their fledgling career: will I be able to keep order in class? One of our challenges as a profession is that we work against the backdrop of a narrative constructed by the media and politicians that we operate in a permanent state of blackboard jungle with unruly children who won't learn, can't learn and don't learn.

We often face the 'hairdresser question'. Well, actually Gary doesn't because he's bald, but Chris does when he goes for his regular perm! Mind you, he's not qualified to comment on how women's hairdressers operate, but if you are a bloke, it often goes like this. You pop down the local high street at 3.30 p.m. to get your hair cut. As you sit down in the chair, the barber whirls a cape around you, soon encircling you in this apparel, before tucking a tissue inside the recently formed collar. We have so far never established the purpose of the tissue, but it is not for us to reason why. That is why this person is a barber and why we teach children. There are doubtless minutiae of our own trade that would elude the hairdressers of this world, not least how you might manage a fractious dinner queue on a wet lunchtime.

As this ritual takes place, the question is asked, 'Half day today, Sir?' Of course, less seasoned campaigners in our mighty profession start to bristle at this point because of an assumed affront to the five grinding lessons which have been taught that day, never mind the marking completed at midnight on top of a parents' evening. Those of us confident that we do a job which most people would make a complete hash of will not be persuaded to rise to the bait, and answer simply, 'No, I'm a teacher.' This will often provoke a diatribe along the lines of, 'Ooh, I couldn't do your job. I mean, kids these days, they get worse and worse. We have them outside the shop, giving me a load of verbal if I tell them not to lean their bicycles against the shop front. They all wear hoodies and half of them have got knives. I would hate to do your job, and there is no discipline these days. I mean, you haven't got the cane nowadays, have you? That's what they need. Bring back the cane.'

Of course, there are a thousand and one things you could say to this person, but given that they are operating somewhere near the jugular vein with some very sharp implements, discretion is usually the better part of valour. You may suggest meekly that teaching is the best job in the world. (Both of us certainly look forward to going to work every single day.)

However, consider for a moment the notion of discipline and how it has developed over the years. Our hairdresser friend is right: discipline did use to be dispensed at the end of a cane. (Have you watched the movie *Kes*? If not, do so.) Fear of the consequences of misbehaviour, which would often involve physical pain, was used as a deterrent to bad behaviour. On the other hand, it probably did more to alienate young people from teachers as a breed, and more potently the whole business of education, than anything else. If you see your teachers as stick-wielding tartars, there to inflict humiliation on their charges, it is hardly going to engage a young person in wanting to learn. We want you to be an 'instrument of inspiration', not a 'tool of torture'.

The conventional narrative which depicts the young of today as being idle, disrespectful and menacing is hardly new.

> The children now love luxury; they have bad manners, contempt for authority; they show disrespect for elders and love chatter in place of exercise. Children are now tyrants, not the servants of their households. They no longer rise when elders enter the room. They contradict their parents, chatter before company, gobble up dainties at the table, cross their legs, and tyrannize their teachers.

This quote is usually attributed to Socrates, but in fact it is actually paraphrased from a 2,400 year old play. Nevertheless, for us, it illustrates the age old issue of how kids have a particular reputation. *Plus ça change.* Oh sorry, that's Chris the language teacher! The more things change, the more they stay the same is what he means! As you enter the teaching profession, you will feel a righteous sense of indignation when young people are denigrated and when our profession is criticised for being ineffectual, mediocre and second rate. One of the lessons you will learn early is that life isn't always fair. Get used to it. The idea that all kids are troublesome is one that will continue to run and run. It isn't accurate, it can be immensely demoralising to people who give their all, often in fairly thankless circumstances, but it will always be there, so take it in your stride. Take a deep breath and get on with being the most amazing teacher ever.

A mate of ours had been working as a teacher for about two months when he met a former minister for education. How this friend came to be in such elite company, breaking bread with the upper crust, can wait for another time. This woman was elderly, diminutive and capable of frightening the wildlife. Our friend explained how she fixed him with a stare through her bottle-end glasses and said, 'Ah, so you want to be a teacher. Have you got your discipline yet?' Frankly, at this precise moment, she had turned his bowels to water with fear, and he didn't think he had anything, let alone his 'discipline'.

So, where do you find this magic elixir? Would it be under D in the Argos catalogue? Is there a discipline tree where teachers pluck the fruit, and hey presto, they have obedience forever? Our mate had no idea, and to be honest, he had only just started out and was teaching children not much younger than himself in a reasonably challenging environment. So, guess what, he hadn't got his discipline yet.

Let's reflect on her question. Think back to your best teacher at school. Why was he or she so good? Chris's was his history teacher and, from the moment he arrived, he and his classmates all worshipped the ground he walked on. Gary's was his chemistry teacher who had the same effect. We would not have dreamt of being naughty or playing up for either of them. Our behaviour was impeccable, our manners unimpeachable and our respect for both absolute from the word go. Neither achieved this devotion with the threat of the cane. In an era when teachers regularly punished children physically, neither of our inspirational teachers laid a hand on us.

Comparing notes, it seems that our super-teachers of yesteryear achieved their 'discipline' by teaching inspirational lessons which absorbed and entranced us and by using a sense of humour to make us laugh. They were also party to every extra-curricular activity going. If we should have been so unwise as to do something which required correction or reproach, neither raised their voice, but the look in their eyes was of impenetrable granite. You never stepped over that line again.

In short, it was all about relationships. We might also reminisce about those teachers we didn't play up because they terrified us. They got in our faces, they shouted, they threatened. These are not the teachers we remember all these years on with any degree of admiration. So, back to the question: who was your favourite teacher at school? Did you play them up? Why not? What was in their locker of skills that commanded such respect and, dare we say it, affection among you all?

TOP TIP

Can you employ these same strategies and tricks of the trade as 'poacher becomes game-keeper' to become an amazing teacher?

The age of dictatorship by fear has gone, the cane has gone, the days of shouting at children have gone. Society has changed the way it defers to authority and, surprise, surprise, so have schools. And they are the better for it. Discipline is, indeed, all about relationships; it should certainly be what your discipline is founded on. So, let's pull this apart a little further to see how it can work for you.

First, let's talk briefly about lessons. Chapter 5 is going to cover this in detail but, in essence, it is very simple. If you don't teach them something they will behave badly. Remember those two fundamental demands kids make of teachers we mentioned earlier? You can probably get away with teaching boring lessons to compliant kids, but if you have a proportion of kids who are not natural scholars, and who make sure that magic tipping point is reached so that they dictate the ethos of the classroom, you will be crucified if your lessons are boring, sluggish, pointless, ineffective or uninteresting. Let's face it, in this age of computer wizardry, TV on tap and non-stop social media, you have to understand what you are competing against.

TOP TIP

When preparing any lesson, you need to consider: (a) what am I trying to teach them? and (b) how can I get them on board?

In this chapter, we are particularly interested in how to get the kids on board. What is the hook? In every child's mind, especially with a new teacher, is the question, 'Why should I work for you?' Sometimes the innate nature of the subject matter will interest them, sometimes they are drawn to and can do the activity you have devised to enable their learning to take place, and sometimes you can create a climate in which it is in their interest to work well. All of these will be looked at in detail below, but it is crucial that you grab their interest. And we don't want to stress you out any more than you already are, but the general rule is that children buy into the teacher rather than the subject, so in the immortal words of Bananarama, 'It ain't what you do, it's the way that you do it. And that's what gets results.'[1]

In order to establish that El Dorado of a classroom where learners are working hard, where there is a good exchange of humour between teacher and learners and where good learning is taking place, your classroom management must be top-notch. This means having the room absolutely orderly and as you want it before the children arrive. There's a very powerful subconscious

---

1   Yes, we realise that, as an NQT, the chances are you're asking yourself, 'Who?'

message going on here; if it looks a mess they will be more inclined to be disorderly and unruly themselves. Organise all your classroom systems so that they are as slick as possible. The devil will make work for idle hands, as the saying goes, so if it takes you too long to do the register, to hand out the books, to give out worksheets or to find what you want on your computer, you are always going to be chasing the game. A rowdy class will lever open your control quicker than you can prise the lid off a can of baked beans. They will be in there like a flash if you are not 100 per cent organised.

Now, remember we mentioned humour. Allow us to digress for a moment. Chris's dad was a naval officer, and when he first went to sea, aged 18, he was given responsibility for a team of thirty hard-bitten, war-weary veteran sailors who worked in the bowels of the ship as stokers and engineers. These were rough, tough diamonds who seldom smelled the salt in the sea air after a lifetime of service below decks. He was wet behind the ears and just out of school. His commanding officer said to him, 'You have six weeks. I want you to know every one of those men inside out, what makes them tick and, most importantly, how to make each one of them laugh. That is called leadership.'

As teachers, we too have responsibility for groups of people. It is our job to be their leader. An American teacher we used to work with was heard to say to her class, 'We are heading west for the Gold Rush. Only I have the map that is going to show us how to get there. Come with me and I will show you the way.' Once you know what makes each and every one of your pupils tick, you will have laid the foundations for that magic thing called 'discipline'.

How can you do this? Use every opportunity for networking with the young people you teach. Every time you encounter one of those children is a chance to touch base with them, to have a mini-conversation which subliminally registers with them that you have taken the time to remember something about them and get to know them. When you pass them in the corridor, when you see them in the dining room, when they pass you on their way in or out of school, a quick comment along the lines of, 'Good Grand Prix on Sunday, wasn't it?', 'Getting any sleep with your new puppy?', 'Brilliant bit of writing you did today', 'That bike looks like a mean machine', is gold dust. This does not have to be a long conversational exchange – it can even be a one-liner before you move on – but, brick by brick, it is helping you to build relationships with these young people, who, in turn, will be much less likely to play you up. It won't be instant, but it will work and it will last.

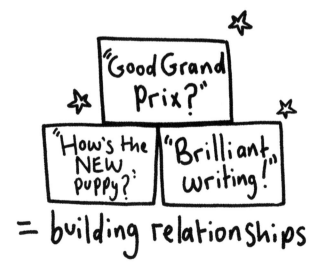

TOP TIP

You can use this technique strategically with those you find the hardest to keep on board. Be courageous and take every opportunity you can to 'accidentally' bump into them. Check out where they will be at break, lunchtime, the end of school or between lessons and just happen to be there with a quip or word of praise. That contact will show them that you care and they will eventually come around.

Playground duty is a great opportunity to catch up with your students. There are those of us who moan and groan about doing duty, but it is the best networking chance ever. Work that playground or dining room. The groupings of children change all the time, even in a twenty-minute break. All thirty members of your least favourite class will not be standing in a group eye-balling you all through breaktime; there will be lots of times when you will spot kids in ones or twos and you can arrange to pass by them and drop in a friendly comment. It all helps to cement relationships. Sometimes you can circulate several times past the same individual or groups of children, throwing in a remark each time. And if you can make them laugh, even better.

Extra-curricular activities are another productive area where you can get involved. When you mix with children at Food Club, Chess Club, Badminton Club, the school play or a trip to the zoo, you will see them in a completely different light – and vice versa. It gives you a currency for your next conversations which will fuel your developing relationship over the next few days and weeks. It enables them to see you in a different light as well, because you are no longer simply the 'new teacher', but the teacher who showed them how to make a scone, return a serve or tell the difference between a cheetah and a leopard. Or maybe you demonstrated an amazing badminton serve, how to win a chess game in six moves or how to sing the first number in the show. We all have our areas of expertise and our party pieces. We once had a teacher who we later learned was a member of the Magic Circle. Did he ever do tricks for the kids? Never. What a wasted opportunity. He could have had the kids eating out of his hands (or pulling rabbits from his hat)! You came into teaching for a whole sack full of reasons, and being a show-off is part of that collection. So, show off, nicely.

Your school will almost certainly have 'special days' where staff are encouraged to dress up or do something daft for charity. Join in. You will be thought of as a good guy and your stock will rise in the eyes of the children as a result. Over the years, our best colleagues have dressed up in wigs and wellies, loud shirts, all manner of costumes for World Book Day and Chinese costumes to celebrate Chinese New Year. Kids love it when their teachers do this; equally, they reserve a certain disdain for those who won't join in. You will certainly drop lower in their esteem if you opt out.

Finally, be prepared to take a risk. If you always play safe, your pupils will ultimately think you are boring, and that is not the basis for the great relationship which leads to great discipline. Jazz up your lessons with something a little bit off the wall, a little bit wow. This needn't be rocket science. A cuddly toy to whom you talk and who can talk with the children is a great asset with learners of any age. An unusual object will always attract attention. It could be a rock, a red wig on your desk or a prop for a child to hold. It could be an imaginary incoming phone-call. It could be a sudden burst of loud music or a funny noise. We each have our own ways of being that little bit different. It all counts. It builds our rapport with our class and then they don't misbehave. That's discipline, folks.

'Okay,' we hear you cry, 'but in the real world there are naughty children and there are tricky classes.' So, let's look now at how to deal with the children who have not yet been beguiled by your magic spell. You have planned amazing lessons, you have tried to network, you have been on the museum trip, but the fact remains, you are having difficulty with a particular class or a particular child.

Start by making sure that you know from the outset exactly what the procedures are in your school for dealing with ill-mannered or naughty children. There will almost certainly be some kind of referral system involving a hierarchy of people to whom you can refer troublemakers and a system of recording incidents. Make sure you learn very quickly who is in the chain of command and how to refer an incident to someone further up the chain. It can be very powerful to mention that you will be having a word with Mr or Miss So-and-So; equally, if you get the wrong name or the wrong person you will immediately lose street cred. It is counterproductive to send a naughty child to the head teacher if the head teacher passes the problem to the year head or deputy head whose job it is to provide front-line support.

Find out what the appropriate sanctions are. What is the normal tariff in the school for homework not done or being cheeky in class? What are the conventions for detentions – are they at breaktime, lunchtime or after school? What procedures should be followed? When dealing with a child who has done something wrong, make sure that you manage it correctly, so you do not find yourself on the back foot and needing to defend yourself (for example, if you shout aggressively at a child, if you don't investigate an incident thoroughly enough to find out who else was responsible, if you overstep the mark in setting a punishment or if you fail to follow school policy). There is nothing more galling than having to back off when it was the child who was in the wrong, not you. Just revisit that Ginott quote in the introduction again. Your discipline needs to be fair; the kids need to know why you are doing what you are doing and what they can do to avoid it happening again.

A word about detentions. Use them sparingly. First, how badly do you really want to spend yet more of your immensely precious time with scoundrels who have already caused you grief? Be kind to yourself. If you do keep them behind at breaktime or lunchtime, always allow them time at the end for going to the toilet and to get a drink or something to eat, and tell them you are going to do this at the start. It will increase their respect for you. If you do decide that an after-school detention is necessary, then find out what your school procedure is for contacting parents. Finally, avoid whole class detentions. You will only alienate the kids who have done nothing wrong and you will have given yourself a much more difficult situation to handle as well.

If you have a challenging class, here is a trick you can use. Always be positive with them. Be at the threshold of your teaching area as they arrive and meet and greet each one as they arrive and settle. This is another opportunity to have a mini-conversation with individuals as they pass you by. Make sure you look each one in the eye – this is a sign of confidence on your part.

TOP TIP

Try using the 'four minute rule' with classes you dread because you have found them difficult to handle. Devote the first four minutes of the session to thinking only positive thoughts and saying only positive words. Come across as a fizz-bomb of energy, a firecracker of enthusiasm and a master of wit and repartee!

As the children arrive, find a positive word to say to every one of them: 'Good to see you,' 'You gave a brilliant answer last time,' 'You're looking very cheerful,' 'I've got a brilliant lesson for you today, and a special bit for you.' Smile and appear as though you are looking forward to the lesson. Do this for the first four minutes and you will be amazed what a difference it makes. Your body language is very powerful. Try it!

TOP TIPS

STRATEGIES TO ENGAGE AND ENTHUSE KIDS AS THEY ARRIVE

- Use your knowledge from mini-conversations when welcoming them.
- Give the odd high-five or knuckle-knock.
- Wear something daft that links to the lesson.
- Sing – play backing music if you can.
- Have a mystery object in your hands. (Gary uses a guitar sometimes, even though he can't play a note – it's a hook to get them wondering!)

Alternatively, try this. Are they actually a naughty class? All of them? Right, so start to sort them out. Who are your solid, reliable good kids who always do the right thing? Cultivate them for all you are worth. Use all your praise strategies with them and have mini-conversations with them in an unobtrusive way (after all, you don't want them to end up being teased as geeks). They are the bedrock on which you can build.

Now identify which ones you need to get in your pocket – the ones who are not conforming to what you want. How are you going to engage them? Focus on your mini-conversations. You may need some background information from last year's teacher, their form teacher or your learning support assistant. What makes these kids tick? Who's into football? Dance? Who's got a new baby in the family? Who's into whatever cult TV programme is the flavour of the month or the latest computer game? You need to get through the outer shell so you can start to build relationships with these kids too.

Luck may also play a part. This works best if you can separate these kids from the rest of the pack, as they then don't have a gallery to play to. If you can catch them on their own going into lunch, at a club or in the playground, then you have a huge opportunity to initiate a genuine conversation where you engage their involvement. Again, use your eyes – your potent weapons! If you are speaking with a child who has been problematic, always separate them from their crime and always accord them your respect. A comment like, 'I rate you, and I want to see you do well. You've got something about you, a bit of character, and I like that,' is coded way of saying, 'You're a bit of a scallywag, but I'm not in the business of wagging my finger at you and telling you off. I want to work with you to make things better.' It is focused on the positive and it opens the door for a constructive dialogue.

Warning! We are going to talk about 'buts' here. Take a deep breath and read on … if you dare. In that last paragraph, it could have gone like this, 'I rate you and I want to see you do well. But …' We don't like 'buts' and we advise you to steer clear of them. As soon as you add the word 'but', it turns a positive into a negative, and what the kids hear is, 'But …' followed by something bad they do.

TOP TiP

Steer clear of 'buts' – all the child hears is 'But …' followed by a negative behaviour.

This applies across your professional life, from every conversation with kids, to staff discussions and parents' evenings. Think of clever ways to keep your positivity focused on what you actually want to see or achieve. Try something like, 'I think you could be good at this, you know. What I'd like to see you doing next is …' And every time they do it, encourage and praise.

It can be a good strategy to put the initial onus on you, as teacher, to make things right, along the lines of, 'What can I do to help you?' This puts the ball in their court and allows a positive conversation to develop. Remember that it is highly unlikely that this child has never been told off before; on the contrary, because he or she sails close to the wind, they have possibly been reprimanded regularly since they started school, and they may well be shouted at continuously at home. They are used to it, so aggressive, confrontational language will get you nowhere. You are trying to forge a relationship here.

Try to get the child to identify what the problem is. It could be shouting out or chatting while the teacher is talking. Once you can agree on the problem, and with some children there may be several (in this case, prioritise – you are not going to solve all of this in one fell swoop), then plan a way forward and, crucially, put in place an agreed reward for achieving the goal. This could be in the form of a merit/star/commendation or whatever currency of reward your school operates. You could offer to have a word with the child's form tutor, head of year or whoever, or even more powerfully, you could offer to contact their parents. Parents of children like these seldom hear anything good about their children. In fact, it is often their parents that these kids want praise from most, so it can be very powerful if you can arrange it.

Gary sent a text home a couple of years ago to a Year 9 girl he taught for English. She had potential but didn't really try. There were no significant discipline issues other than being overly chatty, but she needed a lift. After a week long campaign featuring mini-conversations and the four-minute rule (designed for her but incorporating others to avoid suspicion), he sent a text home praising her excellent effort that week. The outcome was evident the next lesson: 'Thanks for that text to my mum, Sir. She was so pleased she gave me twenty quid!' The girl never looked back and raised her game from then on. Obviously, Gary set up a scheme with her to share the future profits!

TOP TIP

Always praise effort above attainment. You want kids who work hard. The harder they work, the more they engage and the higher the learning.

Does your school have a texting system (Gary didn't use his own phone to send that text)? It is a brilliant way of sending immediate praise to the person who kids most want to know they have done well. We have seen a text home literally turn a student round from the brink. One lad, in the last chance saloon, rose magnificently. He had been to multiple schools and was a constant thorn in the side. His mum rang the school to thank us for the praise text, saying she had never been told anything positive about her son before. That young man hardly ever troubled any of us again. Powerful stuff. Try it.

We are assured that there is a magic number in positive psychology: 2.9013. Well, a ratio, actually, that is most usefully rounded up to three to one. It's called the Losada line and is the absolute minimum of positives to negatives there needs to be for a relationship to survive. And the Losada line applies across the board: at home, work and socially. In practice, it means you have to say at least three positives for every negative. If your communication dips below three to one the relationship will surely struggle. Two important points arise: first, the ratio is not three to none. You are allowed to be critical, so long as it's not your default position. So, please go out of your way to catch kids doing things well and praise good behaviour as well as picking up on bad behaviour. Second, three to one is the bare minimum. It can be argued that when working with children the ratio needs to be seven to one. Please note, we are not advocating rose-tinted false praise, rather a re-engineering of your language to help create flourishing relationships. It's science, so it must be right!

In a similar vein, say thank you. A lot. When you have concluded your discussion, thank the young person for the conversation and wish them luck. Those words of appreciation are a valuable way to gain compliance with a request, particularly with older or sharper kids. You may also find this an effective technique with uncooperative boys. Rather than telling them to remove their cap in class, try saying, 'It would be brilliant if you could remove your cap, thanks,' and walk off. Any lingering intention to stare you out is pointless because you have moved on, and you are more likely to secure their cooperation. Thanking people for the behaviour you would like to see them adopt, prior to them actually adopting it, is a useful way of making people do what you want them to do. And there you have your discipline.

TOP TIPS

TOP DISCIPLINE TIPS

♦ Life isn't fair. People who don't know any better will always say young people are not as well-behaved as they used to be. Get used to it.

♦ Build relationships all the time. Discipline doesn't come from the fear of *force majeure*.

♦ Teach brilliant lessons. The kids won't misbehave.

♦ Make sure your classroom management is as sharp as a weasel's tail.

♦ Make them laugh, preferably with you, not at you.

♦ Use playground duty to have mini-conversations.

♦ Join in extra-curricular activities.

♦ Know the sanctions, but also use the reward systems for good effort particularly.

♦ Speak to the difficult kids without their friends in tow. Always follow things through.

♦ Don't shout at an individual, ever. Be positive. Engage. Make them find the solution and offer to help them. Agree a reward.

♦ Use the four-minute rule.

♦ Get praise into the hands of parents.

♦ Talk about kids positively behind their backs. It will get back to them via the gossip network.

♦ Practise the Losada principle in the staffroom, the classroom and at home.

Chapter 5

One of the fascinating enigmas of our trade is analysing the differences between the way individual teachers operate. There are times when you can watch a group of children in a particular lesson looking bored, listless and prone to misbehaviour. You can then watch exactly the same group with another teacher and they have them eating out of their hand, being perfectly attentive and giving top levels of effort to their work. How come? What is the magic elixir, because if we can identify it with all its constituent parts, bottle it and sell it, early retirement on a paradise isle beckons.

The problem with teaching is that it is an incredibly intricate business. If we have a problem with our car, we take it to the garage, and a very clever person will use a particular spanner to remove and replace a part, and then, hey presto, the problem is solved. Teaching is not like that. There are an infinite number of variables. Teaching an amazing lesson is like doing a thousand piece jigsaw, but you never have all the pieces to hand at any one time. Your challenge is to assemble the ones you do have to the best possible effect.

Chris had a recent visit by his friendly plumber and was dumbfounded by his skill. Within milliseconds he had correctly diagnosed the problem with the cylinder and then set to, dismantling pipes and tubes before replacing them and testing the whole system. Hot water now veritably gushes into his kitchen sink. A miracle. Chris, not known for his practical abilities but actually quite capable, began talking himself down in his admiration for this guy's abilities. He was daunted by the plumber's knowledge and technical skill.

However, it all changed when the plumber asked what job Chris did. He explained that he was a teacher, and now it was the plumber's turn to be impressed. Having briefly talked himself out of having any practical brainpower at all, Chris reminded himself just how skilful good teachers are. Planning and delivering an effective lesson is like weaving a spider's web: it is complex, delicate, painstaking work and requires considerable energy and resourcefulness. If you want any further proof of this, watch next time you have a visiting speaker in school who is clearly not used to spending time with children.

This job of ours is no easy formality. The days of, 'Teaching, you either can or you can't,' are over. Yes, you need to have some innate presence in front of a class, but the rest you learn, day by day, week by week, year by year, and you will never stop learning. One of the joys of being a senior leader who observes lessons is that you constantly learn yourself and come away with new ideas. Take a moment to reflect on how your school works. Is it only senior colleagues who observe lessons? Surely, if you were a brain surgeon, for example, you would learn by talking to and observing other brain surgeons? Teachers should be the same. Every teacher should have the chance to observe other colleagues.

To help us to unpack this puzzle, we need to consult some experts to help us to understand why students behave and work well for some teachers and not others – the kids. We surveyed the students in our school and two factors came through time and again:

1   The lessons are fun and the teacher makes us laugh.

2   There is a variety of activity.

This is a helpful starting point. We have already discussed the question of relationships, and we make no apology for returning to it briefly here. One of the constituent parts of that elusive thing called discipline is humour, making children laugh. If the classroom is a 'fun' place, full of smiles and laughter, and the relationship between the teacher and the children is reciprocal, respectful and purposeful, then the foundation is there for an amazing lesson. Sadly, there are those in the profession who would say, 'I'm not in the business of entertainment.' They are wrong. Think of your classroom as a fun factory that gives birth to learning.

The second ingredient, which received almost universal approval, is variety. Kids like to be surprised, so avoid using the same ritual, the same order of activities, the same use of PowerPoint slides, the same old textbook every time. Think about the fundamental parts of your session. The average attention span for an adult is about twelve minutes. In our case, on a good day, watching a film on TV on a Friday night, it is certainly a lot less. What does that tell us about our children? That they need a mixture of activities during the session and they need the lesson to be chunked down into bite-sized pieces.

Avoid what Ian Gilbert calls a 'fur coat and no knickers lesson', which is very attractive on the surface but lacks substance if you take a closer look. The rhythm of the lesson will depend on a number of variables, such as the age of the children, the nature of the subject, the time of day, the day of the week and even the weather. Nobody outside teaching will believe you if you say that children behave differently in certain weathers. Clearly, they have never been in a school when a thunderstorm has struck, when it is very hot, when it snows or even when it is windy. These things do affect learning, and you will need to adapt your lesson planning to take account of them.

Let's be clear about this. What we *are* saying is that you will need to adapt the way you plan and deliver the lesson. What we are *not* saying is that you devise excuses as to why the children can't learn. There has been a tendency among mediocre teachers we have come across over the years to ratchet up the excuse machine: Oh, they won't learn much in that lesson because …

♦ It's Monday morning.

♦ It's Friday afternoon.

♦ It's the end of term.

♦ It's the beginning of term.

♦ It's wet/hot/rainy/windy.

♦ They've got school photographs/school nurse's visit/rehearsals for the play.

TOP TIP

You can ratchet up the excuse machine and blame the kids, but the bottom line is that you are the 'decisive element' in you classroom and you make the weather. Don't ever blame the kids. You will only succeed in mood-hoovering yourself and others.

You get the picture. Brilliant teachers plan top quality lessons to suit every occasion.

So, how do you start? As we described above, two factors should dominate your thinking as you begin to plan a lesson: what you want them to learn and how you engage and enthuse them.

First, we are going to look at the Learning Aim (we much prefer the term 'learning aim' to 'lesson aim'). It's so important that we are going to capitalise it. The Learning Aim is vital because it provides the benchmark to assess the effectiveness of the lesson, both for the teacher when it comes to evaluating progress in the lesson and, critically, for anyone who is observing the lesson. There is a crucial difference between what the children are *doing* and what they are *learning*. They can be doing badminton, the Tudors and Stuarts or poetry, but in each lesson, what are they actually learning? Is it how to return a serve in badminton? Is it how Henry VIII misused his power? Is it how to use rhythm in a poem?

It is essential for the children to know what they are learning because it signposts to them the direction of travel. This little beauty is not only about the kids though. How do you plan lessons as a teacher if you don't know what you want the kids to learn? Every lesson you teach is about learning and, of course, the children do things to learn. So, you must always start with the end in mind: what will the kids learn?

We suggest that the Learning Aim is shared with class at the beginning of the lesson, at the end of the lesson and returned to continuously throughout the lesson. We often compare this to the sound of waves breaking on the shore. Those waves keep on coming, and so should constant reference to your Learning Aim. There should be no excuse for any child not to know what the Learning Aim is, and every activity in the lesson should relate to it. That means *every* activity. We have both seen lessons with a great all-singing, all-dancing activity as the starter and then, when the Learning Aim is unveiled, it has got nothing to do with what the children have been doing. The lesson should have a continuous narrative, otherwise progress and learning are diminished.

It may seem obvious to say so, but the only prerequisite for a lesson is that the children progress with their learning. Ideally, there should be an identifiable skill or area of knowledge in which they have progressed. So, first base is identifying what you want to teach them. We know that the most important factor in determining how well children progress is the quality of the teaching. This overrides everything else. You can debate the impact of shiny new buildings, a radical curriculum or novel school structures as much as you like, but the predominant factor affecting progress in learning is brilliant teaching.

Second, how are you going to get them on board? Remember the big R? Relationships! We keep coming back to this because it underpins your learning. Put differently, there is an ancient Chinese proverb which refers to wise men catching more flies with honey than vinegar. We explored in Chapter 4 how life has moved on from the days of overbearing force delivering good discipline, and so it is with planning a lesson. It is not good enough to force-feed children with lesson content, telling them that they need this for the exams. Teaching is not an exercise comparable to pouring syrup of figs down their throats, saying, 'You won't like it, but it's good for you.'

The best teachers start from the assumption that their students have zero interest in what they are going to be learning. Surprising though it may be to those of us who have delighted in the academic study of our beloved subject, the street talk in the local chippy is not big on the virtues of iambic pentameter, the intricacies of the perfect tense in French, the capital cities of European counties or the merits of circuit training. You've got to win them over. You've got to make it interesting for them. You've got to get them to adjust their radio dial to W3I's FM, that is WIIIFM (if you're not there yet, What Is In It for Me?).

This the Y generation. They need to know why they are learning what you have to impart to them. The first prerequisite in planning a lesson is rather like those Airblade hand-dryers, the ones which drag your nails from your fingertips and make your fat wobble as they scour the water from your hands. Huge amounts of energy have been injected into the process so that the old days are over of frantically rubbing your hands under a puny current of air, pressing the repeat button at least three times, before in final frustration at the lingering moisture on your hands you resort to wiping your still wet hands on the seat of your trousers. Huge energy; that is one of the secrets (think back to the four minute rule).

Teaching is not and, frankly, never has been for the fainthearted. But now, more than ever, the difference between time-serving mediocre teachers and brilliant teachers, whose class we all would like to have been taught in, is about those who go the extra mile in investing bags of energy into the planning and delivery of their lessons.

There are three key elements to teaching a brilliant lesson: context, connections and praise. We will now focus on each of these in turn.

Context is king, so always try to create a backdrop for the learning. This can be real or imaginary, using kid culture or real-life settings. A science lesson on electricity with a teacher explanation, followed by a brief experiment, followed by completion of a worksheet is okay. However, it will be transformed by the *Doctor Who* music playing as the children come in, a picture of the Tardis on the whiteboard, a clipboard with 'WHO' on the back and an announcement that the Doctor will be arriving in 35 minutes' time and that each group will need to report their findings to him.

Where were you when you heard Diana, Princess of Wales had died? England won the Rugby World Cup? The Twin Towers attack took place? Super Saturday at the London Olympics? We all have memories of things that stick because of the emotion they hold for us. None of the above may be memories of yours, but you may well have others. Try to bring that memory-inducing factor into your lessons.

Chris witnessed a brilliant primary school lesson on the order of the planets. It was given flying speed by the class being divided into groups of four, with each group becoming part of a drama activity where they visited each planet in turn. This lesson was still being talked about four years after it was taught! This takes us on to one of the hallmarks of brilliant teachers and brilliant teaching: they are memorable and stay with the children for ever. Brilliant teachers are the ones we all remember thirty years on, like the history teacher of a mate of ours. He used to do the Winston Churchill voice and our friend still reckons he can hear him doing it now! A champagne moment. An excellent lesson will be remembered, and so will the learning.

A final example: a reluctant group of Year 9s were learning French. The exercise they were doing on answering basic questions was brought to life when they were told that they were in a taxi in Tunisia. The driver speaks no English and doesn't like English people very much. He has given them a price of ten dinars to return them to their hotel. In the course of the ride, the students try out their French. When they arrive at the hotel, the driver charges four dinars instead. Their ability to answer basic questions will save them from being ripped off. All of a sudden, the students had been placed in a context they could identify with and could therefore see the point of what they were learning. The lesson built on this, chunking up the learning with structured tasks, and incorporating fake money, a Tunisian backdrop and even the smells of spices lingering in the air!

From context to connections, the next big tip for teaching brilliant lessons. We have established that however beguiling the content of your lessons might be to you, it is not necessarily so for the kids, what do the children you are teaching do at weekends and in the evenings? Got some ideas? Now you can set yourself the challenge of thinking how you can connect this with what you are trying to get them to learn.

Some great examples we have seen include:

♦ Secondary science: the teacher asked the class to compose a tweet to sum up the difference between an acid and an alkali.

♦ History: the teacher asked a lad what he was interested in, and the answer was Manchester United. The class was studying Henry VIII. When asked how he could connect the two he said, 'The Man United manager needs to be a strong leader who makes tough decisions, just like Henry VIII.' A small connection, but for a United fan it was priceless.

- Primary maths: on the topic of shapes, the teacher gave one of the groups in her class, who were all interested in dance, a differentiated worksheet of dance motifs and asked them how the different shapes were used in dance.

- Primary English: a homework sheet on adjectives was designed for a group of boys who were into football. It featured an outline of a football and they had to fit new adjectives they had been learning into the pattern of the ball.

You will increase your potential to unlock the students' creative energies tenfold if you tap into their own kid culture. Use catchphrases and formats from their favourite TV programmes, refer to big news events that they will identify with, use the names of teen idols or popular mobile phones as group identities, use a variety of caps to identify group leaders – the possibilities are only as limited as your imagination.

As we canter on through how to construct a brilliant lesson, let's not forget about resources. Children can be presented with a plethora of different worksheets in the course of a school day. How can you produce resources that will engage their interest and attention? Remember that you may well be teaching children who do not have very advanced reading skills, so any worksheet featuring a tight block of text will be an immediate turn-off. We recommend that you use at least font size 14 and, if possible, use paper other than white. This may significantly help children who suffer from some learning disabilities. Most importantly of all, break up the text with pictures. These can easily be found on the internet and many are usable without breaching copyright, but do make sure first.

TOP TIP

A very serious worksheet in a recent primary ICT lesson we saw was enlivened by the addition of a kids' favourite cartoon character being part of the action. It is easy to do and goes a long way towards making an excellent lesson. The actual content in this case didn't matter. The mere fact that it included a 'cool' character the kids liked added a little spice to the worksheet and made it more engaging. Try it.

Another useful technique is the creation of an audience, either real or imaginary. A project is given immediate currency in the eyes of the children if they are told that what they produce is going to be used to help learning in, for example, Mrs Pearson's class that afternoon. They can then see a reason why they need to do it. Pride will enter into it, so they will want to do it well, and if a time limit is applied, it will focus their attention.

We described briefly above about breaking the learning down into bite-sized chunks. As the learning progresses through the lesson, it is hugely powerful to have mini-plenaries as you go along. The word 'plenary' suggests something that comes at the end, but it is much more effective to check and assess the progression in the learning at regular intervals, and it is crucial for boys who can have notoriously short attention spans. For a while, the educational world got caught up in three and four part lessons. We say, no way José! Design your lessons in the right number of chunks needed to build up a specific learning narrative for the specific group you teach. You know the group, the balance and their individual needs, so invent your own formula to achieve your goal.

The final major component of a brilliant lesson is the use of praise, which will be key to your success and that of your kids. Remembering the Losada line from earlier, the ratio of positives to negatives needs to be six or seven to one. This means that for every time you have words with a child, you will need to find six subsequent occasions to praise the same child in the same lesson. If you are going to achieve this, you need to deliberately catch them doing the right thing and praise them. The more unobtrusively you can do this, the better, because the last thing a scoundrel will want is to be ribbed by their mates for being teacher's pet.

We can take this a step further. The managing director of a small business we spoke to recently said that it was his mission to speak to every member of his company at least once every week and to praise them. It is the same with a class. You need to be systematic and your praise must cover everyone. Work your way along the rows or round the tables and ask yourself whether you have praised each pupil during this session. If you are not methodical, it won't happen. Some of you will be natural praisers and others will need to learn the habit, but it is a practice worth getting hooked on.

Remember that top tip about praising effort? With effort, everyone in your class can earn praise on a level playing field. Kids are very shrewd and it is no good offering phoney compliments or praise only being available to the chosen few. They will spot a stitch-up in no time if it is only the successful kids who get the acclaim. Equally, they won't be fobbed off with false praise. If you commend them for a painting which is second rate, and they know it, they will reject your praise. It must be genuine and it must be based on effort. Use this sort of praise to focus on the things done well – for example, 'Well done, Will, fantastic effort. Your punctuation is so much better thanks to that hard work. Keep it up.' Make your praise link effort to the outcome and even more success is likely to follow.

Praise is a huge motivator, so you can praise students in advance for what you want them to do or achieve. 'Thank you for getting your book and pen out today as soon as you sit down' and 'Nice to hear the sound of your pens writing with no one talking' are non-confrontational means of securing compliance. They often induce a smile, but even more importantly, the kids do what you want them to do.

Brilliant teachers are extremely skilled in the way they talk to kids. They are assertive without being aggressive. 'If I asked you nicely to remove your coat, would you do it?' typically gets a smile. 'How about if I was horrible and shouted and screamed, would you still do it?' is nearly always greeted with a huge grin and then followed by the child removing their coat. The way you speak to kids is fundamental. If you get in their face, confront them aggressively and see everything in black and white, you will be in for endless bust-ups and unpleasantness, and you will want to retire early. The use of praise before the event gives you another way of going about discipline. Nothing alienates kids more than screechy, bossy, naggy teachers giving it to them in the neck all the time. Brilliant teachers do it differently.

Remember to use whatever the school's currency of reward is for praise. In Chapter 4, we touched on merits, commendations, gold stars, stickers and stamps. They are all great and usable with kids of every age. They can also be used in anticipation – what we call the *premeditated commendation*. This is how it works. Choose your target student who you want to see a change from. Write out and have ready a commendation or reward with their name on it, already dated and ready to give to them. Agree with them what the criteria are for them to win that commendation – it could be making the effort not to interrupt while you are explaining what to do or the completion of a certain part of the task by a certain time. Make the target a short term one. Keep the goals in easy sight. If the child wavers, then show him or her the commendation or reward as a reminder, and when the criteria have been met, give out the promised reward. You can repeat this again and again, stretching and challenging until you have developed good habits. This will act as a huge incentive to good work and good behaviour.

Before we leave our thinking on eye-catching lessons, one last thought: pace and challenge go together. Brilliant teachers judge the pace of the lesson skilfully, challenging the kids collectively and individually. On the one hand, it is counterproductive to try to force the pace unnaturally, particularly if the children feel as though they are being frog-marched from one staging post to the next, without ever really mastering the various steps along the way. The opposite is equally true: if the teacher keeps going over the same thing again and again, it becomes tedious and holds back the learning.

This is where the skilled teacher has his or her finger constantly on the pulse, knowing exactly when to move the lesson on.

You can use various strategies to create pace, such as time limits (fake – they love it when you say daft things like, 'You've got 17.45 seconds left' – and real), movement, individual to pairs to groups and back to individual work, quick tasks mixed with longer ones, watch this, do this, music and competition. Add challenge by telling the group that you think they are capable of great things (the best you have ever taught) and then picking off individuals privately to give them the added belief that they can go further than ever before. You can use the established method of including Learning Aims for all, some or a few. However, you can boost this by encouraging the kids to take a challenge, a leap at learning. They may fail, but by praising them for their effort, they will bounce back and try again: 'You nearly got it that time,' 'Well done, great effort,' 'Keep it going, you'll get there.'

Brilliant lessons: we all remember them from when we were at school (and in education, of course, everyone is an expert because we all went to school.) But brilliant teachers don't just remember them; they deliver them day in day out, so that today's kids will remember these lessons when they are adults.

TOP TIPS

ON EYE-CATCHING LESSONS

♦ Greet and engage the students.

♦ Introduce fun and laughter.

♦ Use variety and chunked-up learning.

♦ Don't be tempted to ratchet up the excuse machine. It's never the kids' fault.

♦ What are they going to learn? What is the Learning Aim?

♦ How will you get them on board?

♦ Exploit pace and challenge.

♦ Create context and make connections with kid culture.

♦ Use praise based on effort.

♦ Design great worksheets.

Chapter 6

QUESTIONING, FEEDBACK AND MARKING

As with observing a skilled practitioner in any area of life, watching a skilled teacher use questions to build learning makes it all look so easy, and yet there is far more to it than meets the eye. A lot of learned theory has been written on great questioning, but we are going to focus on the essentials, because if a brilliant teacher in the making gets these things right, then the rest will surely follow.

First, let's think about the different kinds of question a teacher might ask. The basic type of questioning is about finding out whether the pupil knows the right answer. For example:

What are five 6's?

Comment dit-on 'red' en Français?

Who was Henry VIII's first wife?

What is a simile?

These questions all require a straightforward factual answer and will be either right or wrong. They do not require higher order thinking skills, just knowledge.

This type of question can be differentiated by using alternative answers. For example:

What do you get if you mix yellow and blue?
Purple or green?

In order to differentiate this still further, if you have a pupil who really finds the going tough, rather than say the answer out loud, the pupil can indicate which is the right answer on a prepared sheet, so that you can establish whether they understand the concept, even if they can't as yet say it.

Teachers may also ask questions which they know the child knows the answer to, but the teacher wants them to practise saying the answer to consolidate their learning. This is particularly applicable in foreign languages lessons. For example:

Wie heißt du?

Ich heiße David.

Both the teacher and the child know that his name is David. What the teacher is asking the child to do is practise a pre-rehearsed answer.

A very effective way of consolidating learning is what we call *switchback questioning*, where the teacher asks a question, and then uses the answer to get back to the original question. For example:

What are eight 6's?
48.

How many 6's are there in 48?
8.

If you can generate some pace with this technique it can be very effective, plus you can switch it back repeatedly, adding extra levels each time.

How would you handle different responses – for example, if a child doesn't know the answer? Obviously, you don't want to make the child feel unnecessarily uncomfortable, so don't leave them struggling for too long. It is usually best to move on to someone else, and when you get the answer you were looking for, to go back to the child who didn't know and say, 'What do you think, Naomi? Does that sound right to you?' Give her a smile and a well done. She is now back in the loop.

If you have an inattentive or shy child in the class, it is sometimes helpful to warn them that a question is coming. 'Sophie, I'm going to ask you in a minute what types of rock you might find near a volcano, so have a think and be ready with an answer.' This cues them in so they have a moment to think. Chris went for an interview once and came out quite shell-shocked at the quick-fire questioning to which he had been subjected. Gary gave him precious little sympathy because, as he rightly pointed out, Chris had been subjecting his kids to this form of learning by inquisition for years. (He didn't get the job, by the way. Oh well, their loss.)

This can also apply to the whole class. When you set them a question which requires some thought, give them some thinking time before you pounce. For example, 'What adjectives can you think of to describe how Lady Macbeth felt? Give yourselves two minutes to note down any which come into your mind.' They can work in pairs or more to add variety and cross-fertilisation to their thinking. This will help them to come up with much better answers than if you had gone in cold.

If a child doesn't know the answer, then it can be a very fruitful exercise – one which can boost independent learning – to ask the whole class how to answer the question. For example, the question is, 'What does "philanthropic" mean?' If you invite the class to suggest ways to find an answer, they may suggest Googling it, looking it up in the dictionary or asking someone who knows. The class can then decide which is the best option.

When asked what skills they want future employees to have, employers often say they want creative thinkers; that is, people who know what to do when they don't know what to do. Teaching young people how to do this starts in the classroom at the hands of a very skilled teacher. In national curriculum terms, this is what is suggested by the term 'resilience'. We are charged with encouraging resilient learners. The temptation for any teacher is to tell them the answer, simply because it is quicker. In the longer term, which way is likely to lead to them remembering it? Of course, discovering the answer for themselves.

Once the class have arrived at a correct answer, don't forget the most crucial thing of all: acknowledge all those who have contributed to the process of getting it right and praise them. If you have a gold star, commendation or merit already signed and dated, even better.

One of the skills of really amazing teachers is how they handle wrong answers. These will often come from boys, who will shoot from the lip and give a reflex answer without actually thinking it through. Boys tend to be risk takers. They don't want to have to think, so they will just take pot luck. A brilliant teacher will always acknowledge an incorrect response and thank the child who gave it. Never, ever be sarcastic to a child who gives a wrong answer, and always value the effort that has gone into their response, as long as it is a genuine attempt. If they are trying to get attention by saying something deliberately silly to wind you up, move on quickly and don't give them the showcase they are craving. There is no greater deterrent to a pupil who is playing up than not to get the laugh and the attention they were hoping for.

The most exacting questioning invites students to give a considered response. This requires much more detail from them and will probe higher order thinking skills. Use question stems such as:

♦ Tell me about …

♦ How …?

♦ Why …?

♦ What is the difference …?

♦ Explain …

As the student starts to develop their answer, you can interject with supplementary questions to develop their thinking further.

'The quicker you tell me the names of the planets, the better for you'

Make sure that you spread your questions around the class. Of course, a skilled teacher will know their class and will want to differentiate their questions for different kids. We have mentioned before the idea of a lesson being like a thousand piece jigsaw, and so it is with questioning. Chris remembers teaching what he thought was a wunder-lesson, a veritable cornucopia of brilliance, with Gary as an observer, but was somewhat mortified when Gary said, 'Do you know you ask far more questions to the centre of the room than you do to the corners and the sides, and boys outnumber girls two to one in terms of answering questions?' Chris had no idea this was the case, and it needed an observer to point it out to him.

So, be absolutely methodical in spreading your questions round the class. Be systematic and think to yourself, 'Have I included each child in that row?' or, even better, keep a written record of who you have asked. You may, of course, want a random distribution of questions, in which case you can use the technique Chris saw in an observed lesson recently where the teacher had a cup of lolly sticks with each child's name on a stick. The teacher got a much weaker member of the group, who had been inclined to be naughty, to pick out the sticks. This meant everyone had to be on their toes, and the child who was not previously engaged was now centre stage. Brilliant. There are lots of variants on this theme, and some great random name pickers are available on the internet.

Pick a lolly stick - any lolly stick!!

TOP TiPS

FOR GREAT QUESTIONS

- Think about the different levels of questioning you use.

- Use alternative or switchback questioning.

- Give advance warning of questions.

- Allow sufficient thinking time.

- Help kids to develop thinking skills so they know what to do when they don't know what to do.

- Praise the kid who comes up with the right answer.

- Acknowledge the kid who tried but gave a wrong answer.

- Spread your questions round the whole class so there is no hiding place.

Let's now move on from questioning to two other teaching techniques which our students tell us time and again are the most important in helping them to improve their classroom performance: modelling and feedback.

Modelling means that students have a clear understanding of what 'good' looks like, and crucially how they are going to get there. What steps must they take and what are the criteria for success? It involves demonstrating the thinking process or skills you want them to learn. We have seen it done very effectively in the following ways, but we are sure you can add more to this creative list:

♦ The teacher writes on the whiteboard and describes his/her thinking as the sentences develop. Deliberate mistakes are made and the group is encouraged to spot them. Finally, the group is asked to develop the teacher's work further.

♦ Targeted modelling with a small group or individuals.

♦ Modelling using peers to demonstrate skills.

♦ Older 'cool' students modelling for younger ones.

♦ Invited guests and other teachers as experts.

♦ Differentiated groups, each with a group leader (the modeller) who you have briefed.

♦ Examples from the internet (e.g. audio clips, videos).

♦ Inverse modelling – what not to do. Students point out how to improve.

Once they have started working on a task, the students will need some feedback on how they are doing, what they could do to improve and where they are heading next. For this reason, Chris often refers to this as *feedforward*.

We have talked extensively about praise and its importance in motivating children. It plays a crucial role in improving work and behaviour. Praise is an element of feedback, but really purposeful feedback plays a vital role in developing learning. Feedback comes in two forms: oral and written (written feedback is what we more commonly call marking).

Let's deal with oral feedback first. This is likely to take place during the lesson and, therefore, concurrently with learning. It is the immediacy of oral feedback that gives it its potency, particularly bearing in mind what we have already said about short attention spans, especially of boys. Feedback is most effective when it starts with the positive – for example, praising the child for their effort in what they have done so far – then moving on to giving them tips on how to improve what they have done and how to approach the next step.

Feedback is usually defined as constructive comments from a third party. Most commonly this will be the teacher, but it could equally well come from a learning support assistant or even a peer. If you are going to use peers, then there are some pitfalls to avoid. For example:

Tina, what did you think of Varsha's performance of the poem?

Rubbish.

Why?

Because I don't like her.

If peer assessment is going to be helpful, then it needs to be very tightly controlled by means of precise criteria. For example, you could ask:

Could you hear Varsha?

Did she stumble or stutter? Was she fluent?

Did she pronounce all the words correctly?

Did you hear the rhythm in lines two and three?

This forces Tina to give a more measured and considered answer. This exercise is usually best conducted in pairs or groups and in private, rather than broadcast to everyone. There is one more step to add in here: Varsha needs to have a right of reply. Tina may have given incorrect advice – for instance, she may have said that Varsha mispronounced a word, when in fact she didn't. You need to train the kids to listen properly to the feedback they are given and then consider whether to act on it or not. This can be compared to stopping to ask for directions. You may conclude that the individual didn't know what they were talking about and therefore you won't take heed of their advice.

If well-organised and well-monitored, peer feedback can be a very positive tool. It aids the person giving the feedback as much as the person receiving it, because it helps them to consolidate their thinking about the criteria for 'good'.

Marking a set of books or folders is an extremely time consuming, if vital, business. However, there are some simple rules which will help you enormously when you first begin marking. At the outset, find out what the expectations are for teachers in your school. Every school will have its own protocols and policies. However, what will be common to every school and every situation is that most children will have gone to a lot of trouble to produce their work, and the least they deserve is that their teacher looks it at. They will expect nothing less, their parents will expect nothing less and Ofsted will expect nothing less. Quite rightly. And if you have read it, you owe it to yourself to record the fact that you have looked at it in the child's book or folder. Pages and pages of written work with no indication that the teacher has looked at them is unacceptable. It does happen, but it shouldn't.

Your school should have a marking policy, which might set out how to highlight common errors, such as:

sp   for a spelling error

p   for punctuation

Make sure you know what the requirement is. Every time you mark a piece of work, sign it and date it. That way, no one can ever say that you haven't marked that child's book. Then record the fact that you have done it in your planner. Now, Chris is a dinosaur who still gets a prime-val thrill out of setting up his old-fashioned mark-book at the beginning of every year. In fact, he has been heard wailing and gnashing his teeth under a full moon when a new pupil arrives which fouls up his beautifully handwritten list of alphabetical names. Gary, on the other hand, is a dab hand at all things techie and has used Excel spreadsheets and a variety of apps. So we say, horses for courses. If you like using a tablet or a spreadsheet, go for it. Just make sure it's backed up. The advantage of the techie stuff is that you can down-load data from the school's database and link it to your mark-book. The pen and pencil version doesn't have that ability, but it is flickable and at-a-glance.

Be warned. You may assume that your pupils will master the technique of using the pages in an exercise book sequentially, one after the other. Not necessarily so. Some children find this a tricky concept, and instead simply open a book at random and write on whichever page falls open. You need to clock these kids quickly and put a stop to this. It is sometimes tempting to bemoan their cluelessness, but a glance at your job description will remind you that your job is to teach them, helping them to climb to the next rung of the ladder wherever they start from.

TOP TIP

Ask the pupils to hand in their books open at the right page and organise the books in the order in which you are going to give them out again. You will save yourself a third of your time if you don't have to thumb your way through lots of pages to find what you are going to mark.

So, we have covered the expectations of collecting in work, marking it and recording that you have done so. Job done? Not yet. What should you write in the book or folder? The baseline is that you have written your signature and the date that you marked it. But what have we said about the motivational power of praise? You need to include praise in any marking you do. We both enjoy using praise in lots of different and funky ways to make the kid smile and hopefully to give a nudge nudge, wink wink to their neighbour because they want to show them what the teacher has put.

TOP TIPS

FOR WRITTEN PRAISE

- Souperdooper!
- Yabberdabberdoo!
- Awesome!
- Well done, littl' buddy!
- High five for that!
- Happy days :-)
- A smiley face.
- A google-eyed smiley face.

However, this alone does not constitute feedback. You will spend a lot of time marking, believe us, so it needs to move the learning on. If you simply write, 'Well done, Harrison – good effort', it doesn't. So, what our Ofsted inspector friend describes as 'tick and flick' marking is not good enough. Imagine if this was your child and you were looking through their book. It would hardly impress you, would it?

You need to develop a coherent narrative of developmental comments in each child's book or folder which shows the learner how to progress. Ideally, this should be linked to grades, levels or pathways, so the student knows where they are currently, where they are heading and, crucially, how to get there. This is even more time consuming, so you will not be able to do this with every single child every time you mark their books. Consult the school policy and then decide how often you are going to do this. As a very rough rule of thumb, we think there ought to be a developmental comment about every two weeks, but some may be more detailed than others. Therefore, you might write really detailed comments one week and then, two weeks later, either refer back to this or add another brief comment. You will have to stagger this work, otherwise you will never do anything except mark. Different subjects, carousels on the timetable and practical lessons will all combine to make this more complicated.

It is often a good idea to set students a task to consolidate their learning. So, if they were shaky on their four times table, for example, set them three or four more sums, and then next time you mark their book, check they have done them. It can be useful to do this check-up in a different coloured pen, so if you normally mark in red use purple or green.

We don't have strong feelings about whether you should use red as your normal marking colour. There is some controversy about this, with some saying it is a harsh colour which denotes criticism, but you can make up your own mind on that one. You will also have to make up your own mind, guided by your school's marking policy, on what you correct and how. Clearly, for some pupils, if you correct every spelling mistake you will end up carpet-bombing their work in red pen, which would be entirely counterproductive, so you need to be selective.

Finally, you have invested precious hours of your life marking students' work. But what if they never read it? If they don't then you have wasted that time. So you need to make sure they do read it. Start your next lesson with the books given out swiftly at the beginning (because you collected them in the right order, remember) and give the pupils two minutes' silent reading time to study your comments. Then get them to explain to their neighbour what your advice is. You could then ask the neighbour to tell you. This means they will have to take the time and trouble to read and act upon your remarks.

TOP TIPS

FOR QUESTIONING, MARKING AND FEEDBACK

- Model what 'good' looks like and show them how to get there.

- Always start with the positive.

- Establish clear criteria for peer feedback.

- Find out what the school's marking policy is and follow it.

- Devise a good recording system for your own marking.

- Develop a narrative of developmental comments in children's books.

- Check back to see if they have done what you suggested.

- Make sure they read your comments.

- Use funny praise.

- Make sure your marking is worded so they can use it to improve.

Chapter 7

Pastoral care is a fancy name for looking after kids. When we left teacher training and headed out into the world of education, neither of us had received any training at all in this area. Not a lot has changed in thirty-odd years: pastoral care is still often regarded as secondary to teaching 'proper' subjects. We are going to stick our necks out here and tell you that no school, whatever phase or type, can be good or outstanding unless it has great pastoral care. How well a school looks after its kids and how well it makes them feel safe and wanted is a significant foundation in the children's learning. Without it, it's much harder to create the trust and security needed to lead them into great learning. So, whether primary, secondary or any shade in-between, the pastoral care you impart as a form tutor, classroom teacher or subject teacher is crucial to your success. Get this right and the loyalty the kids give you will be limitless, and it will make the learning happen much more easily.

Here's an example of the bonds that can be created by pastoral care. A couple of years ago Gary received an email asking if he was 'the Gary Toward who used to teach at Sir Frank Markham School in Milton Keynes?' His tutor group from 1983 had tracked him down to invite him to a reunion of the group, thirty years on – and what a night it was! Nineteen of the twenty-four turned up, with people travelling from all over the UK to attend. The power of pastoral care!

I've learned that people will forget what you said, people will forget what you did, but people will never forget how you made them feel.

Maya Angelou

TOP TIP

Copy out the 'decisive element' quote by Haim Ginott from the introduction, and the one by Maya Angelou above, then laminate them and make them into bookmarks for yourself. You might have noticed that we bang on about relationships a lot, but your success as a super-teacher relies on you underpinning all of your knowledge and intellect with the ability to form great relationships with your students and your colleagues. You cannot remind yourself often enough that good relationships matter.

Every day of your teaching life you will be dealing with kids. None of them is your friend or your relative, but if you get your pastoral care right, you will have a significant influence in their lives for the better. Some of your work may become the catalyst that actually takes a child from the brink of disaster to future success. You will share highs and lows with youngsters that may (we warn you) take you through every emotion. We have laughed joyously and chinked glasses celebrating the successes of individual students, but we have both also shed tears about desperate individuals and situations. You are in a career that is about people's lives. If you are as passionate as your letter of application will have said you are, you will make teaching a way of life rather than a mere career.

Your role in supporting children outside the curriculum will focus on two main areas: as a class teacher or form tutor (depending on the phase and the names given to those roles) and as a subject teacher. In both areas, you will have a class full of kids who need your support beyond simply teaching them stuff. So, let's start with the big one, the class teacher or form tutor.

You will be given a group of kids to look after for a year or longer. In some schools, teachers move up with the class year by year; in others, groups move on to a new teacher each year. In primary schools, the class teacher will do the majority of the teaching to one group every day, only passing on to specialists if required by the head teacher. In secondary schools, a form tutor will typically meet with their class twice a day at registration and often for a longer lesson in the week, which can be called all manner of things, but typically is personal, social and health education (PSHE). Careers and sexual education often pop up here too.

If you are a youngster in a primary school class that has one teacher for the most of each day, then you will hope that your teacher understands the need for great relationships. Imagine being in a class for the most of every day over the course of a year with a teacher who doesn't work hard in this area. Similarly, in a secondary school, students want to be able to rely on their form tutor for support when it is needed. It must be very hard for young people if their form tutor sees this role as secondary to their subject teaching.

The second area where your pastoral skills are needed is as a (subject) teacher in general; in the classroom, about the school, on the playing field, on trips – in fact, everywhere you go in your job. Beyond imparting an infinite amount of subject knowledge, skills and wisdom to your classes, you will find there are kids in your lessons who bring with them a wide range of baggage on top of the pains of growing up. Gary's mother was spot on when he got his first teaching job and, despite having no qualifications to validate her statement, said:

> Don't ever forget how you wanted your teachers to make you feel.

Her words resonate with those of Maya Angelou.

It all starts with relationships (yes, we are saying it again because we want to drum it into you!). Pastoral care means, quite simply, caring for the kids, being their metaphorical shoulder to cry on, their greatest supporter in times of need and an inspirational figure of praise when things are going well. In short, you have to be almost omnipresent, a shape shifter. To begin this process you need them to trust you, so do your homework and get to know them – their nicknames, what their dog is called, what they like on TV, whether they have brothers and sisters, what they like to eat. All this lovely ammo gives you a vast range of starting points for mini-conversations. The subliminal message is that you like them, understand them and respect them. If you don't believe us, you might believe Dale Carnegie. His seminal book, *How to Win Friends and Influence People*,[1] was written

---

1   Dale Carnegie, *How to Win Friends and Influence People* (London: Random House, 2006 [1936]).

in the 1930s and the big message that shines through is that if you want to create high quality relationships, you need to be *genuinely* interested in other people. So, although the times have changed, we reckon that the secrets of how to build rapport have not.

We are now going to take a quick detour into names. In your career, you will come across a smorgasbord of children's names, some typical and unremarkable, some unusual and unexpected. By your fifth year of teaching, we predict you will be giving advice to your friends on what not to call the baby they are expecting ('Whatever you do, don't call them @£$.?&. They are always naughty'). You will learn the thirteen different ways we have seen to spell Chelsea, and you will even start to invent your own versions. Above all, you will wonder why anyone in their right mind would come up with some of these names.

QUICK QUIZ

Which of these have Chris and Gary taught over the years?

- Theresa Green
- Scott Land
- Annette Kertain
- Paige Turner
- Gladys Friday
- Barbara Seville[2]

---

2 Between us we have taught Theresa, Scott, Annette and Paige. Had we been much older we might also have taught Gladys and Barbara, as they are both genuine names.

Before we move on, let's just sort out this business of whether or not we like our students. You may have heard a colleague say, 'I'm not paid to like the kids.' Well, we guess not, but neither are teachers paid to dislike the kids. In fact, you are paid to be positive. We've got a whole chapter on this coming up (see Chapter 8), but in a nutshell you are paid to inspire kids and to teach them stuff, no matter what kind of pain in the backside they can be at times. Goodness knows how many thousands of kids we have taught or come across in our years at the chalk face (crikey, that dates our travels; maybe it's digital face now), but we can't think of one who would have spent hours dreaming up ways of cheesing off their teachers like some sort of master criminal. Most of the unpleasant aspects of young people can be put down to a few things: their home life, the transition from childhood to adulthood plus a smattering of peer pressure. You can pretty much guarantee that if you understand the relationships business, and work hard at it, then any hassle you get will never be personal.

Being a great classroom teacher or form tutor can make you stand out and add bonus points to your status in the school. Teachers who understand their kids pastorally are easily picked out by leaders because, surprise surprise, the kids talk about them behind their backs. Make it your personal mission to give them the best deal possible. Treat them like your surrogate family and be proud of them. Be disappointed not cross if they mess up, celebrate successes with them and mentor them collectively and individually to create strengths from areas where they are weak. Give them something of you, your personality and individuality, and they will respond in kind.

You might hear this phrase (we've heard it hundreds of times): 'I blame the form tutor.' It's usually said in jest, but in actual fact, it's not the children's fault that they are always late for assembly, or that they don't get the bulletin read out to them, or that they haven't got a full team for the inter-form Ultimate Frisbee Competition. The best tutors and class teachers lead their groups so well that their charges develop a glowing and fierce sense of pride and identity, and would go to the stake for their class and teacher.

TOP TIPS

FOR BEING A BRILLIANT CLASS TEACHER OR FORM TUTOR

- ◆ It's never personal if the kids get it wrong.
- ◆ It is up to you to be the best tutor you can be.
- ◆ Create routines for the group.
- ◆ Give roles to individuals.
- ◆ Create competition within the group.
- ◆ Set up a group reward scheme that supports the whole school scheme.

- Support individuals.
- Communicate with parents about good things. The only contact should not be because a child has made an error.
- Liaise with parents for support.
- Organise class events – a weekly quiz, student of the month, class picnic, competitions, reading, sums and challenges.
- Praise the group systematically for the things you want them to do.
- Praise individuals publically and privately.
- Thank them for things.
- If you are feeling poorly, tell them honestly – they will support you.
- Always support them at inter-house/ inter-form competitions. Help them to organise for it.
- Set up supporters for these events, even cheerleaders and special chants.
- Get involved in additional meetings about individuals.
- Mention students who need support/ understanding in staff briefings and emails.
- Give each child a birthday card and a Christmas card.
- Tell jokes and create class sayings and standing jokes.

Be the BEST you can be...

Some of these tips can easily be applied to your general teaching too. They all work and are tried and tested strategies.

Pastoral care continues further afield – around the corridors and classrooms, playing fields and changing rooms. It never stops. Use all of these situations to create and develop relationships. You might be the new kid in town, but how else can the children get to know you away from your classroom if you never venture out? Just going for a walk once a week to see what is going on will give you opportunities to meet and greet. We know a young colleague who makes it her mission to take a different route to and from her classroom each time she is away from it, using those opportunities to engage with kids and staff. You never know what might come from going that extra mile.

There used to be a series of books when we were kids, *I-Spy* guides to … creepy crawlies, wild flowers, flags, ancient Britain. They have been updated now and are still great fun for kids, but there isn't one for teachers. That is how we see this book. If we were to write an *I-Spy* on teaching, it would have to be in several sections, but the most important one would be pastoral care. Here are our suggestions for what to 'spy' for:

- The mood of a child. Is it different to normal?
- How the child looks. Is anything different? Are they dirty? Unkempt? Unhappy?
- If they are normally organised, are there signs of being disorganised? Homework not done? Lateness? No PE kit?
- Is the child not with it, unfocused or not concentrating as normal?
- Is a normally calm child displaying temper or anger?

Your school will have a safeguarding policy and procedures, so your first port of call is to follow those guidelines. Super-teachers spot these warning signs and follow through for their kids.

Yes, *their kids*. You will, if you get this right, be using those terms. Remember, you have not just bought into a career. This is about changing lives for the better.

The MAGIC Ingredient

Chapter 8

THE MAGIC INGREDIENT

Whatever you do, above anything else you read in this book, if you have the magical ingredient, you will have the most crucial quality for a successful career in teaching. But what is it?

Before we start, here is a story to set the scene. In our lofty positions of senior management, we gaze down occasionally and watch the world of teaching go by. Ofsted and other inspection-minded folk call these 'learning walks'; we think of it as knowing which way the wind is blowing. It's no different from settling down in your favourite cafe by the big bay window and watching the world go by; except we do it and see the same people, observe how they are doing, how they are working and how they are developing. It's people watching with a purpose. We see the ups and downs of life in teaching, often in a microscopic way, but more than anything, we see what it takes to succeed.

There is one common denominator to success: positivity. We have seen it create brilliant teachers from the start of careers and mend stuttering or broken careers.

TOP TIP

The magic ingredient is something we can all choose to have: positivity.

Our mate, Andy Cope, is a guru of positive psychology. Where much of psychology looks at what goes wrong, positive psychology looks at what makes things go right. What we are going to describe here isn't rocket science, but it can help to make your career and your private life incredibly fruitful. Put simply, what Andy has found, after years of research, is that the people in this world who are positive choose to be that way. It's not genetic, and nor is it determined by the weather, political change or congested roads – we all have to face these annoyances. By combining our anecdotal research with Andy's more scientific approach, we reckon you need this little bit of magic too.

Fruitful

'It's all very well you two saying that it's a choice,' we hear you cry, 'while I'm here juggling three piles of marking and Declan has just punched Jake in the back of my classroom. I'm not feeling full of the joys of spring.' Yeah, well, that's just tough, isn't it. Here's the news, folks, hot off the press: teaching is a hard job and things don't always go to plan.

Let's look at it this way. Not only is it helpful for your career, your kids' learning and your personal life for you to choose to be positive, but we propose that it is actually part of your job to be positive. Even if your day begins with cleaning up the disembowelled remains of a mouse left by your cat and is followed by you accidentally bumping your new car into a bollard in the car park, your kids deserve a teacher who shines, not a teacher who snarls.

Now we've got that clear, let's look at positivity in more detail. How do you manage it? One of the issues for you, and also for the rest of us Brits, is that we aren't exactly rocking the world when it comes to seeing the bright side of life. Just take a look at the news, which is typically dominated by stories of doom and more doom, apart from the final story about Josie the blackbird who has made her nest in a cement mixer's engine bay and has halted work on the footings of a new superstore.

Even worse, some of the newspapers love a good whinge about education, and really crank it up at the end of August when the GCSE and A level results come out. It will make you feel so valued each year when you learn that the rise in higher grades and the number of students being successful is because of easier exams and isn't anything to do with better teaching or the efforts of students! As a nation, we just love a good moan. Probably while queuing up for something.

QUIZ TIME

1 Which, according to surveys, is the happiest country in the world?

   a Australia

   b Denmark

   c Vanuatu

2 Where does the UK come in world happiness league tables?

   a Eighteenth

   b Tenth

   c Forty-first

---

1 Answers: (1) Depending on which survey you look at, all these countries have appeared at the top of a world happiness league table, although it seems that Denmark is the most consistent. (2) The UK has been placed in all of these positions, depending on what survey you look at. We thought eighteenth didn't sound too bad, given how many countries there are in the world (196 for the pub-quizzers among you), but as an example of the negative spin of much of the press, it was reported by one newspaper as 'only eighteenth'. (3) Generally speaking, the further north you go in the UK, the better it seems to get. Harrogate and Sheffield have both been reported as being the happiest places to live. Sadly Leicester hasn't, although we both love it.

3 Where is the happiest place to live in the UK?

    a Sheffield

    b Harrogate

    c Leicester[1]

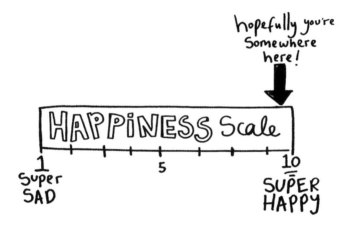

Where are you on the scale of happiness? The UK average is currently 7.3, by the way. Positive psychology boffins would call that your 'set point', and they would also tell you that it was your baseline, which stops you living in a euphoric 10 out of 10 or a depressing 1 out of 10. But we like working with Andy because he reckons it isn't 'set'. He calls it your 'familiar point' and, with a little practice and modicum of hard work, you can raise it by twenty per cent. And here's the really brilliant news: your emotions are contagious, so by raising your happiness by twenty per cent, you are automatically influencing those around you. While we don't want you to have so much happiness that you are leaping down the corridor, doing handsprings and hurling daffodils in every direction, you should understand the impact of your state of mind on others. Basically, Andy's simple science informs us that how you are, what weather you bring to school (and life) will affect your kids (and beyond). Choosing to adopt a positive approach doesn't mean you always have to be a cheery soul – you are allowed to have challenging times. But if you join the two per cent of the UK population who sit on the happy chair for most of the time, you will bounce back from those hard times and your students and family will feed off your positivity. You will be what Andy calls a two per center (2%er). We love that!

There has been a great deal of research into how to develop constructive habits, but by and large you need to deliberately and systematically make yourself kick out the negative vibes and adopt new positive habits over a period of about five weeks. Knowing yourself and being honest (even asking others who know you, but be pre-pared for stuff that might hurt) will help you to identify the mood-hoovering aspects of your personality, if you have any.

All we'll say to finish this chapter is that being a 2%er takes effort, but, boy, is it worthwhile!

Chapter 9

COLLEAGUES

Depending on the size of your school, you will have anything from a couple of colleagues in a small rural primary school to over 100 in a large secondary. In either case, your colleagues matter to you and you matter to them, whether you know them personally or not. This is because you all belong to the same team, and the team is only as good as its weakest member. So, let's make sure that isn't you.

If you have read Chapter 8 on positivity, you will have no doubt chosen to be a 2%er. So, by now you are fully equipped to be a great member of your new team. Your first job is to learn who the team members are, what they do and what they are like, while also sussing out team tactics and protocols. We have covered much of this already, but here is the extra bit.

You will need to make what we describe below fit to your personal circumstances but, generally speaking, this is about the dynamics of the team. Your key function in this team, first and foremost, is to make sure that you do what you should be doing. Mostly this applies to being in the right place at the right time, consistently applying school policy and managing your workload. It's a no-brainer really. No one wants a colleague who doesn't turn up for their breaktime yard duty until the last five minutes, and then only after there has been a punch-up between Sam and James, and Mrs Beaton, the catering assistant, has caught Kaylee trying to nick a piece of flapjack, while someone else has run into Mr Snidgepodge, the caretaker, as he's trying to clean up some spilled milkshake. The first question a school leader will ask is, 'Who was supposed to be on duty?' In reality, most schools would function perfectly well without lots of close supervision of kids, but given the nature of the beast, if there is going to be a catastrophe, it will be when you are late for your duty, even if you are usually on time.

The same can be said about the rest of the 'should be doing' list – basically, what is called your job. So, if there is a policy that says you mark your books every two weeks, make sure you do so. And don't leave it to your memory. You are going to be busier than you have ever been in your life, so plan ahead. But what if you don't do your marking? Does this really affect your colleagues – after all, it's just between you and the kids, isn't it? Okay, imagine you heard that a colleague wasn't marking his books. How would you feel? How does it affect the kids? Some of these by now will be 'your kids'. What will the parents think? It all adds up to poor teamwork.

We could rattle on about this a lot but we won't, because we think that if you have got enough about you to have leapt into this great profession of ours, you will want to make sure that you become the best teacher you can be and will get those basics in place. Mind you, you will need a game plan for the times (which will arise, we assure you) when you have a week with two parents' evenings in it, you've got a cold and your car needs new tyres. If you are having trouble with deadlines or any other matter, talk to someone about it – usually your line manager, mentor or head teacher.

So, assuming you have all the basics taped, you can now build on your bedrock and begin to assume super-colleague status. Being good at what teachers are supposed to be good at is all well and good, but to be brilliant you need to take the next step – as the band, Madness, put it, 'One step beyond …'

TOP TiPS

FOR BEING A SUPER-COLLEAGUE

- ♦ Put the kettle on and offer to make drinks.
- ♦ Bring cakes on your birthday and/or randomly.
- ♦ If you know someone is feeling unwell, offer to do their duty.
- ♦ Similarly, if you are not teaching, offer to cover their lesson while they take a breather.
- ♦ Share resources you find online by email.
- ♦ Share other resources by 'show and tell'.
- ♦ Offer help and support to colleagues.
- ♦ If you make a display that is easily replicated, do a copy and share it.

- Praise and thank your colleagues for ideas you pick up from them.

- Refer to teachers as 'teachers' and staff as 'staff'. Do not refer to teachers as staff.

- Organise a social event, either in your department or wider.

- Thank your cleaner, caretaker, receptionists and other support staff who help you with cards, chocolates, beer, etc.

- Go out of your way to help colleagues in need (e.g. a colleague has bus duty and it's pouring with rain). It doesn't pay back every single time but we assure you that most colleagues will return the favour in your hour of need. That's how high performance is created.

- Head a team or volunteer some support on the sports or arts front.

- If you see a colleague alone with a parent at the end of parents' evening, hang around until the parent has gone.

And one bonus tip for when you are a bit more established:

- Have a laugh and play a few practical jokes – let the kids in on it too.

We would like to think that all of this will set you up in the important world of mutual back-scratching. Your box of chocolates will pay you back tenfold when you need a bit of support from reception with a difficult parent, and putting the kettle on will open up all sorts of useful professional, social and spiritually supportive alliances. Furthermore, people talk about great colleagues behind their backs – the right sort of talking. It will get back to you, and most importantly it will also get back to senior staff, who are always on the lookout for people with positive qualities.

Staff in schools are, generally speaking, a microcosm of the rest of society. The bigger the school, the broader the mix. For the purposes of this book, we are being deliberately stereotypical, simply because we can't deal with every variation of person in every school role. Nevertheless, you have to learn to work professionally with them all.

Let's start at the top with head teachers. Gary's had a bit of experience here, so we are going to tell you what makes them tick and how to handle them. The head teacher, the head, the boss, that ; there are several names for the person who is in charge of the school. You will probably find yourself using all of them during your career.

In the past, old school heads were seldom seen or heard by staff or kids. Gary tells this story of his headmaster, as they were called back in the 1970s. Gary had been attending the school for seven years when the headmaster, with black gown billowing behind him, stopped Gary (who was 18 at the time) in the corridor and asked him the way to the boys' toilet. You might think that in a rough mining area of the north-east, the gown would have been the issue that took Gary aback, but you would be wrong. This was, in fact, the first time he had seen the headmaster in the corridor and also the first time he had ever spoken to him. It seemed that the plumbing in his en-suite had broken.

Today you can expect a much more mobile and communicative head, but bear in mind that a head's focus is often not the same as yours. With responsibility for a big budget, £5 million plus in a large secondary, and ever changing pressures from government and inspection regimes, being a head is a stressful job. Having said that, get a feel for your head from your colleagues. Are they chained to emails or do they wander the corridors? Are they approachable to staff and students? They should be all of these things and more but, like all professions, you will find totally different approaches.

We have found that the majority of teachers want two things from a head teacher: firm discipline with the students and support for all staff in doing their jobs. Most also want heads to deal with any slackers on the workforce too, although that isn't usually said in public. Heads generally make it their business to know what is going on across the school, which is why you need to buy into the team spirit, as discussed above. Essentially, what a head wants from their teachers is a good classroom practitioner and someone who supports their students. The team game comes next, and then it's down to what extra you do to add value to your school.

It's a good idea to deliberately bump into the head teacher early on, just to remind them who you are and that you have arrived. From then on, make sure you speak to the head regularly; tell them what you have been up to and share anecdotes, just like you would with any other member of staff. Above all, don't see them as a distant ruler in an ivory tower. You need to interact with them. If you notice the head passing your classroom, invite them to step inside. In fact, when you do something a bit special – a particularly exciting and explosive chemistry lesson or the final of a maths competition you have been running – invite the head to come along. Let them see you at your best and engaging with the kids.

Some staffrooms are hives of activity, others have tumbleweed blowing through them. Each school differs. If your school has a busy staffroom you need to make sure you spend some time in there without becoming a fixture. You will probably find a few fixtures in there, though, as most schools have someone who likes to hold centre stage or has a particular chair that he or she has sat in since the last ice age. Don't sit in the chair!

We know of a few cases when teachers like these have cheesed off their colleagues to such an extent that their chair has been sabotaged. The most dramatic incident in Gary's career happened to a particularly large woman who regularly held court and put down any upstarts with her vicious wit. One

day, in mid-tirade about some hot topic in the school, the back legs of her chair cracked, sending the woman flying backwards, legs akimbo, next week's laundry on show to all. Close inspection of the chair later revealed several saw marks near the point of the fractures …

The key to mastering the busy staffroom is to pop in, check your post (as it's usually in there), chat politely to those who catch your eye, discuss the kids, chew over the latest news and make small talk, but don't become part of any 'put the world to rights' staffroom committee. You need to target and form bonds with creative, positive and enthusiastic thinkers like yourself, while making sure you are pleasant and polite enough to earn the respect of the others.

In small schools, you could be on a staff of just four or five, but you need to manage this in just the same way. With any luck you will find that, because of the size, the team is particularly cohesive and positively like-minded, but be prepared to play the small talk game to avoid any mood-hoovers.

Your line manager, head of department or mentor will hopefully be an inspirational character in your career. Let's hope they haven't got the charisma of the person this quote was written about:

His men would follow him anywhere, but only out of morbid curiosity.

Comment on appraisal form

If you find that there are similarities and your leader opens their mouth only to change feet, then you need to find someone else quickly to be your inspiration. What you don't want is to pick up any negative traits. However, most people in school with responsibility for any form of staff development are selected because they are good at it, so you should expect to be inspired and for there to be an open door for support and advice.

There will be other incredibly inspirational people in your school too. You will spot them easily because others will look up to them. The heliotropic effect, like sunflowers following the sun, works just the same, and you will often find several teachers feeding off the seemingly natural and radiant positivity these people radiate. Join the followers and soak up the glow; it's infectious and you want to catch it.

Remember our top tip about staff meaning all staff. Well, it's not just about what you say; it's about who you work with. Your relationship with support staff in their various guises – teaching assistants, receptionists, business managers, caretakers, cleaners, catering staff, technicians – is crucial. Many of these individuals will be locals who know what is happening in and around the area and will, with the right encouragement, report this in kaleidoscopic detail. Such intelligence can be worth a mint if you are trying to get to the bottom of why one of your tutor group is always tired; the librarian might tell you she sees him in the park next to her house every night at 10 p.m.

In the same way that great pastoral care underpins the academic learning of the school, great support staff are an integral part of the team. You need their respect and you need their support. They have incredible power, even if their job title is not so lofty. A colleague told us about the school he once worked in, where the person who was in charge of reprographics was both a great bloke and also held great power, because his role meant he was the sole person responsible for bulk copying and printing in the school. If you wanted something fast, he was your man, but only if you had his respect. So, those teachers who were, in his opinion, of poorer standard and also paid support staff less respect, would wait longer for their printing.

It shouldn't work that way, but human nature dictates that if you want a caretaker to fix the blinds quickly in your room, it is wise to make sure that the cleaner who is responsible for your room isn't complaining behind your back because you leave the window open every night or that the floor is a mess. This takes us right back to that mutual back-scratching. So, if you go on a staff night out, make sure that you mix with the support staff too. They will respect you for it. Small tokens of thanks and kind words during the year and at the end of term can pay dividends too. Remember, support staff will earn less than you do, but because of personal pride in their job and loyalty to the school, they will often go well beyond their hours to help the kids or you.

We have discussed the importance of corridor contact and mini-conversations with kids, but it's equally important for you to reach out to your colleagues. Teachers are full of busyness. There is a lot to fit in during the day and just travelling to the loo can happen in a rush. So, smile and say hello to colleagues as you pass them. Goodness knows how many times we have heard someone bemoaning, 'He'll pass you in the corridor as if you weren't there.' These little things matter. They show your colleagues that they are important to you and will help to build up that mutual respect and team feeling.

During any week you will also come into contact with supply teachers, educational psychologists, nurses, police ... the list goes on. These people are your colleagues too. They are direct partners of the school, sometimes contracted and sometimes associated by interest (e.g. social workers); therefore, you need to treat them as you would any member of staff. They will all form views of you and the school from the way you interact with them and how they see you interacting with students and other staff. It all matters as they will, without doubt, pass on their views outside of the school.

Recently Chris visited a school in another local authority to do some training. While being guided to the room where his presentation was to take place, the senior person leading him passed four members of staff. None of them spoke to his guide and his guide didn't speak to them. None spoke to Chris either. No wonder the head had engaged him to do a day's workshop on positive teamwork.

Finally, a bit like the cloud, somewhere out there in your school is a governing body – the governors. In most schools these folks are diamonds. They work for the school without pay, yet are often criticised by the government which wants 'professional' governors but doesn't want to pay for it. These individuals come from all walks of life. Many are parents or ex-parents of children at the school. Some are there by previous political appointment through the local authority. All will want to do their best for the school. Mind you, not everyone can give the time needed to reach the standard the government wants or the school needs. In our experience, most governors do it to give something back to society or the school. Few are in it because they have to be (for example, their company has a community commitment or because they have an axe to grind and want to put their four-penneth in).

Governors are responsible for school policy and they also oversee standards and finances. In the case of academies or self-governing schools, they are likely to be your employers. Treat them as you would any of senior staff – with respect, welcome and collaboration. If they are visiting the school, engage with them as you would the head teacher, perhaps taking the opportunity to invite them to anything special you have going on. Just because you don't see them, don't make the mistake of thinking that they don't matter.

There you go then. You are part of a team, but your role in school goes well beyond the classroom. How you interact with your colleagues can be a game changer in your career.

Chapter 10

PARENTS

An experienced colleague was once heard bemoaning the approach of a Family Fun Day at school with the words, 'I thought my job was to educate the kids. I didn't realise I was supposed to educate their parents as well.' Well, strictly speaking our esteemed colleague is right, although the Teachers' Standards do make reference to engaging with parents.[1] But what he was missing in his casual cynicism was that he could be denying himself a powerful way of engaging with his students. Yes, we are focused on the kids, but kids have parents whose attitudes have a massive impact on them. Engage with the parents and you increase the child's chances of doing well at school. It's in our self-interest as teachers to do so. There's an old African proverb that says, 'It takes a community to raise a child.'

We have long nursed our own private theory about this, and now we are going to share it, so I guess that means that it isn't private anymore. There is a magic tipping point in a class, somewhere around a third

---

1   Department for Education, *Teachers' Standards: Guidance for School Leaders, School Staff and Governing Bodies* (London: DfE, 2011; introduction updated June 2013). Available at: https://www.gov.uk/government/uploads/system/uploads/attachment_data/file/301107/Teachers__Standards.pdf.

(depending on other variable factors as well), where once you have the parents of that number of kids actively engaged in their children's education, it alters the whole tone of the class.

The Department for Education and Skills recognised this back in 2001 when they referred to parents being 'key partners'.[2] In 2007, this had become, 'Parents and the home environment are the most important factor in shaping children's well-being, achievement and prospects,'[3] and later to, 'Parents' support for children's learning is an essential foundation for achievement.'[4]

Recognising the impact that good parenting can have on children's attainment and progress at school is vital for every teacher. The next step is knowing how to tap into this immensely powerful resource. Parental engagement is necessary but, if we may sharpen our focus for a moment, the role of fathers is particularly important, especially for boys in an age where it has become increasingly prevalent for kids not to have a resident father. Many studies tell us that a father's involvement during a child's upbringing is a key indicator of their subsequent progress at school. Active father

2 Department for Education and Skills, *Schools Achieving Success: White Paper* (London: The Stationery Office, 2002). Available at: http://files.eric.ed.gov/fulltext/ED465856.pdf.

3 Alan Johnson's foreword to Department for Education and Skills, *Every Parent Matters: Helping You Help Your Child*. DFES-LKDA-2007 (Nottingham: DfES, 2007). Available at: http://webarchive. nationalarchives.gov.uk/20130401151715/http://www.education.gov. uk/publications/standard/Parentscarersandfamilies/Page4/ DFES-LKAW-2007.

4 Department for Children, Schools and Families, *The Children's Plan: Building Brighter Futures*. Cm 7280 (Norwich: The Stationery Office, 2007). Available at: https://www.gov.uk/government/uploads/ system/uploads/attachment_data/file/325111/2007-childrens-plan. pdf.

engagement leads to a reduced likelihood of low educational outcomes, criminality and poor life chances. Furthermore, fathers who get involved by reading with their kids and supporting their education boost their children's chances of doing well. So, try to make a concerted effort to engage with fathers (we will suggest how to do this later in this chapter).

Of course, you are probably thinking that this is all just good common sense and confirms what your native intuition is already telling you. If so, jump in, cast a lifeline to all those parents out there and reel them in. It probably won't be so straightforward in practice though. There are myriad reasons as to why parents are not always easily persuaded to engage with their child's school. At the outset of your career, have a little barter with yourself. Put a pound coin into a jam jar every time you hear someone say after a parents' evening, 'Of course, the parents of the kids I would really like to see didn't turn up.'

It's all too easy to descend into a diatribe about feckless parents who don't care about their kids' education, but we have never yet come across parents who don't care about their children. We have, however, come across a lot of parents who find it very difficult to engage with the school. That is very different. It is probably no surprise that the families we find hard to reach, in turn, find school hard to reach. It doesn't take long to unpack some of the possible reasons why:

- Negative personal experience of school.
- Negative experience of being a parent if their child is naughty or not very able.
- Feeling of being out of their depth among professional people.
- Lack of self-esteem which makes them think they have little to contribute.
- School jargon.
- Transport – can they get to the school?
- Childcare issues – are they available at the times we want to see them?
- Shift work – are they available at times which suit us?
- Health issues – absent parents are often absent because they have health issues of their own.
- Communication – do they speak English?

If we put ourselves in their shoes for a moment, it is not hard to see why the parents we most want to see are often the ones we see least often. One parent put it like this: 'I have been coming to school since Dylan was 5, and all I have ever been told is that is he is behind, that he is cheeky and naughty, with teachers telling me what a nightmare he is.' You might give up engaging with school too if this was your experience. So, if you are a brilliant teacher, how do you deal with issues like these and learn to deal with parents effectively?

Let's start with parents' evenings – a golden opportunity to meet the power behind the throne. We have never come away from a parents' evening without having learned something useful about a child. If you are lucky enough to stay for a stretch of time in one school, you will begin to get to know the local dynasties as subsequent siblings cross the threshold. It is always a light bulb moment when you are talking to a parent, and suddenly the penny drops, and you realise that the child you are talking about is the sibling of another child you have taught. It can be very misleading because it is quite common for children's surnames to be different, but it comes back to relationships once more. Use parents' evenings to build relationships.

Being able to enjoy mini-conversations when you encounter parents again, either at the school show, watching a sports fixture or in the local supermarket, is gold dust to you as a teacher, because it subliminally transmits the message to the child that it isn't worth trying to play teachers off against parents, or vice versa. And if their dad thinks you are a good teacher, then they had better work really hard for you. Treat parents' evenings as a privilege and use them as a means of raising the performance of your kids and helping them to learn better. When it's a dark January evening, there's snow on the ground, you're not feeling your best, you've had a full day's teaching, you've got marking to do and a family member is poorly, remember that parents' evenings rock!

TOP TIP

It is by no means unknown to get collared in the check-out queue at your local DIY store or supermarket (Gary seems to find parents queuing up for him at the broccoli section in the supermarket for some reason!). After extending niceties, do not feel obliged to talk in detail about their child's progress or listen to their latest whinge about the school. This is your private, off-duty time. You can be quite polite in saying, 'It's really important that we have a proper chance to talk about this. Give me a ring in the week and I will see what I can do for you.'

TOP TIPS

FOR GETTING THE MOST OUT OF PARENTS' EVENINGS

♦ Think about your appearance. Parents are expecting a professional conversation about the most important person in the world to them, and they regard you as an expert. Look smart, be smart.

♦ When they arrive at your desk, stand up, look them in the eye, shake their hand confidently, introduce yourself and invite them to sit down. This first encounter is crucial in setting the tone.

♦ Treat them as equal partners in their child's education. As the teacher, you will contribute a lot of the expert knowledge, but they have huge expertise in their child. Draw on it, ask them what they think you can do to help their child further, make them feel important and not preached to. A great way to start the conversation is to ask them an open question, such as, 'How do you feel about his/her progress?' This puts them in the box-seat.

♦ Always be positive. Yes, always. You may want to offload some bile about a difficult or challenging child, but if you have a student who is giving you grief, the last thing you want is a disgruntled parent who says to their child, 'I can see why you don't get on with that teacher.' Look for solutions, not problems. If the child is not where you want them to be, how can you move them forward? What can they suggest? Empower them to come up with ideas.

♦ Prepare, prepare, prepare. Make sure you have all the data and examples you need to hand. Tell them where the child is in terms of their progress. This means using school jargon (i.e. grades or levels), but make sure you explain to them what the number or letter means. How does it compare to their peers? How does it compare with where you would expect the child to be? What do they need to be doing next to move on? If it is appropriate, have examples of the child's work available. Remember, praise is much more powerful than criticism if you want to achieve better work or better behaviour.

♦ Give parents practical ideas as to what they can do to help their child. Parents often say to us, 'We want to help our child but we don't know what to do. It was easy at primary school, but we are out of our depth at secondary school.' This could be very simple advice – for example, to ensure they have PE kit on a Tuesday. Alternatively, it could be to suggest that dad reads to (or with) them. We have found that when fathers read with their children, especially with boys, it can have a significant impact. Parents have often said to us, 'We want to help our child but we don't know what to do. It was easy at primary school, but we are out of our depth at Secondary School.' More examples will follow.

♦ Be ready to refer them to someone else if you don't know the answer. This can be done on the evening itself or you may want to buy time and have a word with one of your colleagues in the morning. If you do this, always undertake to get back to the parent within a specific time frame (e.g. 'I will get back to you by the end of the week'). Make sure you do.

♦ Offer to keep parents in the loop. If you have a student who is not on track always offer a follow-up contact date (e.g. 'Shall I give you a ring at the end of the month, because by then we should have noticed a difference?'). This comes across as very professional. It also sharpens the mind of the child, who realises that this is not the end of the matter, and it is much appreciated by parents.

♦ If you have a parent who is in danger of over-running, do not be afraid to say, very courteously, 'I'm sorry but I will have to move you on now because, as you will understand, I have other appointments.' Then offer them another time, if that is appropriate, or pass them on to someone else if they have a serious concern about something.

♦ If you have a parent who is being deliberately awkward or difficult, do not hesitate to summon help from a senior member of staff or another colleague. It is perfectly professional to stand up and say, 'I know who will be able to help us with this, and if you would excuse me for a moment, I will just see if my colleague, Mrs Brown is free.' At either end of the parents' evening, always make sure there is someone else around. Equally, if you have finished and your colleague is still busy, it is really supportive if you can stay until a senior member of staff appears.

♦ To close, stand up, shake them by the hand again and, most important of all, thank them for their time. Even better, go one step further and send them a text via the school office next morning thanking them for coming in.

We promised you some more ideas on what parents can do to support their children's learning. These apply to any age and any subject, so cherry-pick the ones which suit your parents and pass them on at appropriate times.

TOP TIPS

FOR PARENTS

- Read together – especially dads with lads. It doesn't matter what you read. It can be fiction, newspapers, magazines, articles on the internet, cereal boxes … anything. Read together and talk about it together. Ask them what they think, whether it triggers any memories, what they think will happen next, why something you have read about has happened? Also let your child see you reading. You are their most powerful role model.

- Take an interest in everything your child does: their friends, their hobbies, what they are doing on Facebook, what they have done in English or maths or geography. If they have had triumphs, celebrate with them, however small they might be. It could be something as simple as they stopped a squabble between two friends, they understood something for the first time or they spoke to a visitor in school. It doesn't matter: share the champagne moment.

- Listen. Parents are busy, especially in big families, but multitasking is a speciality – and, yes, dads can do this as well. Make time to listen, and let them know you are listening. If they are telling you something, it is because it is important to them. If you can't listen at that precise moment, tell them you want to hear what they are saying and postpone your listening, but give them a time and a place so that they know they aren't being fobbed off.

♦ Be there when things don't work out. Again, listen and help them to find a way forward together. Don't preach, don't boss, don't nag. Work it out together. Always, always be positive.

♦ Talk together. What is one of the biggest impediments to children's development? The fact that roughly half of UK families do not have a dining table. What do families do around a dining table? Eat, yes … and talk. It is vital for children's language skills that they interact and talk with other human beings, not just via a screen on social media. Talk with them as you go about your everyday activities – walking, driving, shopping. Talk to them; don't just bombard them with questions. This is a conversation not an interrogation.

♦ Homework. Make sure you know when it is set and when it should be handed in. Guarantee quiet time and an uninterrupted place for your child to study. Organise the use of the family computer. (Give them ideas as to what to do when their child is stuck.)

♦ In response to the question, 'I don't know anything about physics or French, what can I do to help?', explain that they can turn this to their advantage by getting their child to teach them about the mysteries of mass and density or the perfect tense with *être*. Make the child be the teacher.

Remember, this is a partnership of equals. Parents actually quite like being referred to as the experts – after all, they have known their child since day one. Good communication helps to forge a balanced relationship between parent and school, one which will be very much to the benefit of the child.

Chapter 11

BUILDING YOUR CAREER

A few weeks ago, Gary made the keynote speech at an NQT conference. As a build-up to introducing Gary, the organiser of the event asked the audience if any of them had ambitions to be a head teacher. Several NQTs raised their hands. At the same time, Gary noticed that there were looks of amazement directed at the hand-wavers, the odd nod of approval and some blank stares. Luckily no one ran screaming from the room.

Like it or not, you are on a career path, and like any good path it has its twists, turns, hills to climb and meandering valleys. You may already have an ambition to progress to some form of leadership. Or you may not even have thought about it – for now, your main goal is just to get a job and survive the next year. There is no right or wrong answer. Both of us have climbed up the ladder of leadership. At the start of our careers, though, neither of us had paid any attention to that at all. We just wanted to teach and teach well.

However, career development is not just about new jobs and new roles. It's about becoming the best teacher you can be, and from our experience that process never stops. We both still teach, but even after more than three decades of being classroom practitioners we still learn new things, often from the newest teachers in the school. The key to being a brilliant teacher is never to stop being a learner yourself. It won't come from going on courses. It will come from your own desire to learn and from using your creativity and networking skills to constantly reinvent and scavenge new approaches. You will need to take risks, crash and burn, then bounce back with a different approach. If you hang on to that desire, that passion, you will be brilliant and your career will continue to flourish.

Just being a teacher is not an option for super-teachers. While you might want to simply teach, by the very fact that you want to be great at it, you will not be able to avoid getting into situations where you take the lead. It doesn't mean you have to be a head of department or a literacy coordinator, but having applicable skills and experience will mean that opportunities come your way. (Yes, extra work is an opportunity!) You might be asked to write a scheme of learning, to lead on developing a whole school policy or mentor a new teacher. These things will happen, not because you have strategically planned for them to happen but because you have created your own fate. By being so good at what you do, you will become the obvious choice for that role or task. Whatever you do, don't think that you can be a great teacher and take a back seat. Being a pastel shade in a school won't help you or the kids. You need to shine like a Van Gogh palette in order to be that teacher whose lessons all the kids enjoy.

We talked about your shop window earlier in the book. Officers in the First World War stopped dressing like officers when they went over the top as they became a target for snipers. You, hopefully, will do the opposite and make sure that the right people see you doing things well. You will have played the 'pick me' game. Your currency will be high within the school and beyond the school gates, with parents, governors and local colleagues (who you will begin to meet with if there is good liaison in your area).

TOP TIPS

SOME SIMPLE STRATEGIES TO GET AHEAD IN THE 'PICK ME' GAME

♦ Make your classroom vibrant by using creative and inspirational displays that you change regularly.

♦ Take your learning outside of your classroom – for example, displays in the corridor and teaching in the yard, hall, field or corridor.

♦ Dress up occasionally as a character from a book, from history or someone relevant to your lesson.

♦ Sing to your class as they enter (even if you're tone deaf, you can still mime to Beyoncé!).

♦ Always keep a focus on your kids. Talk about them with colleagues and mention individuals you are concerned about in staff briefings.

- Volunteer for trips, visits and extra-curricular activities.
- Write about things your students have done and post it on the school website.
- Write an occasional article for the school newsletter.
- Share your kids' successes with colleagues and parents.
- Offer to take the minutes in a meeting or two.
- Represent the department or the school at a local meeting.
- Provide some training for colleagues – for example, you might be good at certain new techie things that your colleagues haven't had time to keep up with or grasp.
- Take photographs of events and display them.
- Play the team game.

At some point, you may decide that you want to dive into the leadership pool. There can be all sorts of good reasons for this: maybe you have been inspired by a colleague or woken up in the morning after a great dream (steady on), you might fancy a new challenge or may have dipped your toe in the water and liked it, or you may have said to yourself, 'I can do it better than him.' But whatever you do, don't get promoted into a post just because you want more money. If remuneration is your motivator, then you won't bring the right attitude to the role and it will undermine your career rather than enhance it.

Going back to that NQT conference, the clear ambition of some individuals suggests that it is worth considering how, providing you are doing all of the right stuff that makes you stand out, you can plan world domination … or at least aim to move up the rungs on the ladder towards senior leadership.

First, let's look at the routes. Traditionally there are two: curriculum and pastoral. You can try both if the opportunities arise, but be aware that they require different skills, time commitments and workload demands.

A curriculum leader typically means being in charge of a certain area of the curriculum. A first rung on that ladder might be a temporary post to develop or lead a strategy or a role that involves oversight of a whole school initiative. Later on, you could move on to being head of a subject area, head of department or head of faculty (depending on the school). All of these roles will demand that you are well organised, have creative vision and can inspire others. You will also need to spend many additional hours monitoring, evaluating and planning, although a lot of this work can be done away from school.

The main pastoral roles are head of year group or section of the school. In contrast to curriculum positions, these roles mostly add to your in-school workload as they tend to be supportive, problem solving roles. This means there is often very little you can do to plan ahead – if there is an issue, it just needs to be sorted. This can be full-on, intense and emotional work.

Straddling these two traditional routes is another option that combines aspects of both, special educational needs. You might find that you enjoy and are particularly good at supporting students with individual learning needs. Specialising in this area requires all of the skills and demands of a curriculum leader as well as those that fall within the pastoral domain. If you find yourself drawn to this area of education, there are several different types of special schools where you could develop your career.

Building experience helps in all of these cases, so look for opportunities to develop your skills and illustrate that you have potential. David Campese, the brilliant Australian rugby union winger, used to say that if the ball didn't come to him, he would go looking for it. This attitude made him one of the most prolific try scorers in the game. So, don't wait for things to arrive at your doorstep – hunt them down. Walk into the head's office and ask if there is the possibility of, for example, helping with the development of how data is used to improve teaching and learning or managing a particular section of the school's website.

If you are really up for promotion then you may have to consider moving schools. There are various degrees of choice in this area and between us we illustrate them well. Chris started out in London, moved to Staffordshire, then to Leicestershire and from then on stayed in the area, moving schools for promotion to head of department and then, in the same school, to assistant head. Gary, on the other hand, was promoted in his first school, then moved to Norwich to a head of department post, then to Sunderland to a head of faculty post and then to Leicestershire for a deputy headship. He stayed in Leicestershire and became head of that school.

So, there is no simple answer. You just have to make your own fate by applying for jobs within the parameters you set. One thing to bear in mind if you do move schools is that you will have to build up your status once more from scratch. None of the things you have done in your first school will travel ahead; you will have to earn respect all over again. There will be new kids and new staff just waiting to be impressed by you.

To conclude, let's consider performance management. It has, over time, been called all manner of things – from appraisal to personal development – and no doubt it will change again. But it all boils down to one thing: your professional development within the professional standards established by government and schools.

In your NQT year, your focus is to complete the year successfully. We were called 'probationary teachers' when we started and had to impress our line managers in much the same way. After that, you step onto the performance management ladder and will meet with your line manager yearly to establish targets, review past ones and to discuss other aspects of your professional life. Each school will have a slightly different way of doing this, but by and large it focuses on meeting professional standards and developing any weaker areas. Typically, your targets will be set along the 'weakness' lines, but we strongly advise that you go to any meetings with some suggestions of your own. If you are a reflective teacher, and hopefully you will always be, you will do this naturally.

Targets can cover any aspect of your professional standards, so think carefully about what will make a real difference to what you do in the classroom and around the school. Have an eye on this during the last few months of your NQT year and hone in on your personal developmental needs. Quite often, schools will want something related to the professional standards as a key target, but they also may have agendas of their own that the school leadership team has highlighted as a whole school weakness and will want every teacher to focus on. This could be marking or numeracy across the curriculum, for example.

You may also be asked to have a target for additional training. This might mean that you take part in some in-house professional development or participate in a training event that is happening locally. You may even be sent on a course. If there is a clear gap in your department or area of the school – for example, if you are in a primary school and there is no one with expertise for assessment of speaking and listening – then you could volunteer and set it as one of your targets.

Beyond this, keep tabs on the standards for the upper pay spine. If you are heading for promotion, we suggest that you track yourself against those standards to ensure you meet them.

TOP TIPS

CAREER TICK LIST

- ♦ Take on a responsibility in the school or department for no extra pay.

- ♦ Look for gaps that need plugging and offer to address them.

- ♦ If you have ideas, share them.

- ♦ Be honest with yourself about your skills and expertise.

- ♦ Make it your mission to improve on any weaknesses you have.

- ♦ Be ambitious about your career as a teacher and, if you choose, as a leader.

♦ Make sure your performance management targets challenge you and make certain you meet them.

♦ If you feel yourself getting too comfortable, make some changes to challenge yourself. This may mean moving schools or areas.

Before we finish, we would like to expand on that last point because you may find it a bit off-putting. In your career, it's likely you will come across teaching staff who are very negative and/or cynical. We've even met teachers who have made a strange career choice considering the fact that they don't actually like children! Luckily they're not abundant, but one is enough for us. Be careful of these people. Smile politely. Tolerate them, but please don't find yourself agreeing otherwise you might find yourself sitting in the same staffroom chair, sipping from the same mug, bemoaning whoever the education secretary happens to be in ten years' time. The truth is that some people are more alive than others. The key to staying fresh in your thoughts and practice is never to think you've cracked it.

The sigmoid curve is a helpful little beastie. It's a nice graphic illustration of why change should be made even if things are going well. It's typically applied to businesses, but it works well for individuals too.

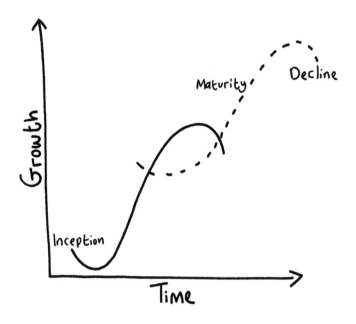

Apply the diagram above to your career. In your first few years, your 'growth' in teaching will hopefully be rapid and sustained – a steep learning curve, as they say. You will continue this growth rate but eventually your learning will begin to slow, and if left untouched it will eventually plateau. It is at this point that there is the distinct possibility that it could go beyond the curve and begin to dip, and you will unwittingly begin to dress in brown corduroy and sensible shoes. If you find yourself groaning at every new initiative and sighing when changes are proposed, it's time to move on.

Will Ryan sums this up very well in a cool little story in his book, *Inspirational Teachers Inspirational Learners*. A mood-hoover teacher is grumbling to the head teacher, 'You've only been head teacher for five minutes and you come here criticising my classroom practice … You seem to forget I have thirty years of experience at this school.' To which the head teacher replies, 'No, Mrs Jones, you have one year's experience repeated thirty times.'[1]

Our point? Don't become that teacher! You need to catch yourself at the point of plateauing and use change to reinvigorate yourself. This can be as simple as changing classrooms, subject specialisms or taking on a new role, but it may need to be something more radical. Talk to people you trust, people who will give you honest feedback, and tell it as it is.

You have joined a great profession. It has huge challenges but the rewards more than compensate. Keeping a positive head on your shoulders is going to be fundamental to your success. You will have ups and downs and you will need to bounce back from difficult situations. You will get things wrong, but you will get much more right. Sadly, you will never ever know what difference you have made to your students – it's impossible to tell – but in our experience it's huge. In fact, we would go as far as saying that it's life changing.

We'd like to say good luck, but that wouldn't be right as luck doesn't come into it. Be brilliant instead!

---

1 Will Ryan, *Inspirational Teachers Inspirational Learners: A Book of Hope for Creativity and the Curriculum in the Twenty First Century* (Carmarthen: Crown House Publishing, 2011), p. 75.

Chapter 12

We hope you are looking forward to your career and, even more, we hope you have found some useful stuff in this book to help you. Oh, by the way, did we tell you that if, by any chance, you become a megastar in the field of education (although it's not down to chance; it's down to you and you *can* do it) the small print of this book states quite clearly that you will have to buy us a beer. Just so you know well in advance, as we are looking forward to it.

So here is our last top tip. It might be that you are feeling daunted by a new job in a new school. And you're going to be worn out during the first year, because every one hour of classroom delivery takes four hours to prepare. The great news is that things do get easier with practice. But if you are having a crisis of confidence or you think you just can't do it, play our little holiday game. All you have to do is send your unconfident doubt-ridden personality on holiday for two weeks. They have gone, far away, leaving you the opportunity of being your absolute best self. If you really enjoy being brilliant, you can always email your negative self and tell them it was a one-way ticket!

We can't finish without another bit from our mate, Andy. You should have worked out by now that the business of staying positive will give you the foundation to become a brilliant NQT and then a brilliant teacher. (This, by the way, is a blatant plug: please do go out and buy our other book, *The Art of Being a Brilliant Teacher*.[1]) So here you go. Take it away Andy …

---

1 Gary Toward, Chris Henley and Andrew Cope, *The Art of Being a Brilliant Teacher* (Carmarthen: Crown House Publishing, 2015).

Brand you

Righty-ho. That's it then. If you have got this far and absorbed the lads' words of wisdom, your NQT initiation will be less stressful than it would otherwise have been. But, in the interests of grounding you in reality, the next couple of years are going to be exhausting. You see, it's not just the day job of engaging the hearts and minds of young people, it's the whole life encompassing thing that teaching happens to be. If you do it properly, that is.

So, if I may, I would like to finish with some top-notch stuff from the realms of positive psychology. Brace yourself for some eclectic top tips on happiness, change, self-belief and hotel chains.

Most people have a wait problem (and, no, that's not a typo). They are *waiting* for an opportunity to feel good. In fact, I have never met a profession that suffers from such a happiness 'wait problem' as teachers. Tens of thousands of teachers are *waiting* until half-term to be happy.

Quit waiting! Nobody has to wait to be happy. It's almost as though 'happiness' is some sort of mythical pot of emotional gold, positioned tantalisingly at the end of the rainbow. It's 'over there' somewhere. You will be happy when you get observed as outstanding. You will be happy when you have finished your marking. You will be happy when you have survived your first term. (Tell me when I'm boring you.) You will be happy when you have befriended Connor, the 'lost boy' from Year 9. You will be happy when you have delivered your first whole school assembly …

You need to learn to be happy *now* (although I appreciate that it is not quite as easy to do as it is to write). You see, happy people perform better. They are more creative, more energetic, more positive and they create strong personal relationships. Have you ever wondered why Chris and Gary have had such success?

But happiness in the now can be difficult when the pressures are intense and some of your colleagues are stuck in moan-mode. The chances are you will hear a lot of teachers complaining about 'stuff'. Mostly the complaints will revolve around workload and change. The truth? The workload is immense and change is manic. Just like every other job in every other sector! Have a chuckle to yourself when you twig that those who complain the loudest could actually reduce their workload if they stopped moaning and got on with being positive. (That's a private little chuckle to yourself, mind, making a mental note never to become that person.)

As for change, avoid the very common habit of thinking that change is a six month 'thing' to be gotten through. You are a teacher. Your job is to change people for the better. Change is what you do. It's forever.

Here are a few things you can do to boost your happiness levels.

First, write a list of ten things that you really appreciate but take for granted (having a job might even be on your list). Keep the list by your bed and take a peek at it every day. You lucky b******.

Lucky b****** list...

1. I've got a roof over my head.
2. I've actually got a wife!
3. I love my playstation.
4. I have a car (Its not A Bentley but it gets me from A to B!).
5. I get paid to have 13 weeks holiday a year!!
6. I have 2 kiddies that mean the world to me.
7. The lads invite me out for A beer.
8. The pub is less than ½ a mile away.
9. My job is pretty enjoyable.
10. I'm ALIVE!!

When I was doing my teacher training I was given the advice of 'don't smile until Christmas' (this gem was given to me by some doddering, old, unsmiling failed teacher who couldn't engage kids so had sought a few 'easy years' delivering teacher training). So, second, I'm giving you the opposite advice. Smile from day one. It's not a nicey-nicey pushover smile; it's a warm, friendly, quietly confident, approachable smile.

If you have ever stayed in a Ritz-Carlton hotel,[2] you will notice what they call the 10/5 principle. The 10/5 means that you smile at everyone who comes within ten feet of you and make eye contact and say 'hi' to everyone who comes within five feet of you. It boosts your confidence, it makes others feel good and it doesn't cost a bean!

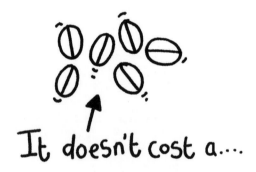

It doesn't cost a....

Finally, self-belief. Being new in any job is daunting. Being new in the classroom and staffroom, especially so. Hopefully you will join a thriving department full of awesomely supportive people, and you will feel right at home from the start. But you might not. In which case, please remember that your self-image is merely a belief. It's not real. Your self-image is an idea that has been

---

2 No, me neither. I'm more of a Travelodge man.

formed over the years. The image becomes imprinted on your subconscious and takes on a life of its own. You end up believing it. You *become* your self-image. So make it a good one. If you don't feel particularly confident, act confident. If you don't feel very happy, act happy. Hopefully you won't have to resort to faking it too often, but sometimes, *ahem*, faking it is okay.

And, while I'm on the topic of smiling, did you know that happy people are luckier than miserable people? That is a massive subject for another book on another day, but the chances are you are already very lucky. For example, I know a head teacher who, when recruiting for new staff, bins half of the application forms without even looking at them. His motto is that he doesn't want to employ an unlucky person!

To conclude, I'll leave you with an activity (homework, oh joy!). In thirty years' time, there will be a school reunion. The children you are currently teaching will all get together for a shindig. The beer will flow and there will be laughter aplenty. It will be an evening of reminiscing about boyfriends/girlfriends, pranks and school trips. But most of all the conversation will be about teachers.

What do you want them to be saying about you?

GLOSSARY

This little list of educational terms, abbreviations and acronyms is to help see you through the foggy depths of jargon you will come across. You will never know it all and this doesn't even scratch the surface, but it's a helping hand … Oh, apart from the spoof one we've thrown in to keep you on your toes.

A level	advanced level
achievement	the progress made by a pupil
added value	the progress pupils make
ADHD	attention deficit hyperactive disorder
attainment	the standard a pupil has reached (e.g. in an assessment)
AWPU	age weighted pupil unit (used in allocating school finances)
banding	portions of students organised on the timetable by similar ability
base line	the starting point to measure progress from
BSP	behaviour support plan
BTEC	Business and Technology Education Council
CAT	Cognitive Ability Test
CPD	continuing professional development
DBS	Disclosure and Barring Service

DfE	Department for Education
DT	design and technology (sometimes includes A for art)
EAL	English as an additional language
EDS	excessive daytime sleepiness (you may find this in period 5)
EFL	English as a foreign language
EIP	Education Improvement Partnership
EP	educational psychologist
FFT	Fischer Family Trust (a group that analyses performance data)
FSM	free school meals
G&T	gifted and talented
GCSE	General Certificate of Secondary Education
HLTA	higher level teaching assistant
HMI	Her Majesty's Inspector
HoD	head of department
HoF	head of faculty
HoY	head of year (or year head)
IEP	individual education plan
IIP	Investors in People
improvement plan	a timed targeted plan with success criteria to deal with weaknesses
ITT	initial teacher training

JPD	joint professional development
KS	key stage (can be 1–5)
LA	local authority
LAC	looked after children
LSA	learning support assistant
MFL	modern foreign languages
NEET	not in education, employment or training
NoR	number on roll
NPQH	National Professional Qualification for Headship
NQT	newly qualified teacher
Ofsted	Office for Standards in Education
P1	period 1 on the timetable
PAN	planned admission number
PE	physical education
performance tables	published league tables of data of schools' results
PM	performance management
PP	pupil premium
PRU	pupil referral unit
PSHE	personal, social and health education
PTA	parent-teacher association
safeguarding	child protection procedures in schools
SAT	Standard Assessment Task

SEN	special educational needs
setting	classes grouped by ability
SS	social services
TA	teaching assistant
UCAS	University and Colleges Admissions Service
VAK	visual, auditory and kinaesthetic
VLE	virtual learning environment
WIIIFM	what is in it for me?
Yr	year (can be 1–13)

RECOMMENDED READING

Tait Coles, *Never Mind the Inspectors* (Carmarthen: Independent Thinking Press, 2014)

Andy Cope and Andy Whittaker, *The Art of Being Brilliant: Transform Your Life by Doing What Works For You* (Chichester: Capstone, 2012)

Richard Gerver, *Creating Tomorrow's Schools Today*, 2nd rev. edn (London: Bloomsbury Education, 2014)

Paul McGee, *S.U.M.O. (Shut Up, Move On): The Straight-Talking Guide to Creating and Enjoying a Brilliant Life* (Chichester: Capstone, 2005)

Ken Robinson with Lou Aronica, *The Element: How Finding Your Passion Changes Everything* (London: Penguin, 2010)

Matthew Syed, *Bounce: The Myth of Talent and the Power of Practice* (New York: HarperCollins, 2011)

Gary Toward, Chris Henley and Andrew Cope, *The Art of Being a Brilliant Teacher* (Carmarthen: Crown House Publishing, 2015)

Here's our website – we'd love to see you at our courses and workshops, and we'd be happy to visit your school:
www.decisive-element.co.uk

And Andy's website:
www.artofbrilliance.co.uk

ABOUT THE AUTHORS

Chris and Gary come from completely different backgrounds but both have developed a similar passion for teaching, and between them they have over seventy years' experience in the classroom. Both fizz with energy and crackle with creative ideas for engaging kids.

Chris trained as a French teacher in London secondary schools before taking up his first post in an 11–18 comprehensive in Tamworth, and then moving on to Leicestershire. He moved to a middle school to take on more responsibility as a head of modern foreign languages, eventually becoming assistant head of an 11–16 academy. Between those last two posts, the true luvvie in Chris came to the fore and he led the school's specialist status as an arts college, a key aspect of the school gaining an Ofsted grade of outstanding. This also involved teaching in partner primary schools. Unsurprisingly, he has turned his hand very successfully to teaching drama too, and has written and directed school productions with casts of up to 170 students.

Gary started in the north of England and yo-yoed around the country from Milton Keynes to Norwich, to Sunderland and back down to Leicestershire. He is a design technologist by trade but eighteen years ago, after plugging various gaps in science and humanities, he became a permanent fixture in the English department, teaching at top primary and secondary level. He continues to teach English as a head teacher. During the last fifteen years, he has been head of the same secondary school but has also led two others, the latter being a pupil referral unit which he (alongside colleagues) took out of special measures.

Chris and Gary are both highly experienced teachers, with success both in the classroom and leading teaching and learning. Their company, Decisive Element, is one of the country's most popular for workshops, keynote speeches and inspiration. So far, they have put around £100,000 into their school's funds, financing further developments and resources for students.

Outside of education, Chris is a keen cricketer, walker and amateur thespian, while Gary plays football, skis and climbs mountains.